AWAKEN YOUR ALPHA

TALES AND TACTICS TO THRIVE

ADAM LEWIS WALKER

AWAKEN YOUR ALPHA

RƏTHINK PRESS

First published in Great Britain 2018
by Rethink Press (www.rethinkpress.com)

Cover image 'Galaxy' © Shutterstock/Triff

PRAISE

'This book should be required reading for adolescent boys, high school boys, college-bound men, working/professional men and retired men. There is not a man alive who wouldn't benefit from reading and implementing what is contained in this magnum opus.'

PAUL EDGEWATER
CEO Busy Bee Promotions, author and marketing expert

'I'm pumped up, motivated and my testosterone is turned on! I'm ready to challenge myself and take action, today. Right now. *Awaken Your Alpha* appeals to men truly interested in bettering themselves. Nothing is promised. However, as a man – a real man – you can change your life with a single committed decision. Never take no for an answer when you're faced with adversity and perceived overwhelm. Read this book, now!'

PJ DIXON
Motivational speaker; life, love and relationship coach

'Adam has spent the best part of the last five years interviewing people at the top of their game with one simple goal: to code success. Week in, week out, Adam has not only scoured the earth looking for the most successful men, he's interviewed them. After 300 episodes, the patterns and common denominators are now captured in one place and you are going to love the result. No matter what you are facing in your life, be it problem or question, this book is bound to contain the answer or solution. A must read for the modern male who wants to operate at their best.'

JOHN BLAKE
Sales expert and founder of Sales Breakthrough Solutions

'Don't be kidnapped by your impression, each man can achieve greatness and happiness at the same time. Adam not only lived through the anguish of hitting the reset button on his life, he allowed himself the time and space to analyse it to answer a burning question and passion that he was born with. Adam firmly makes his stand to clearly research this topic, while he guides you to understanding the importance of each of us making the time to take our own stand. Thanks for sharing this, Adam! Awesome.'

REG LENNEY
The multi-award-winning Vital coach and author of *Be You*

'Adam Lewis Walker has put together a *stonker* of a book. Full of his own insights and stuffed with anecdotes and lessons from amazing alpha minds, this book will help you *Awaken Your Alpha!*'

JACK TURNER
Hollywood leading man: *My Summer Prince, One Winter Weekend*

'When it comes to awakening your alpha, Adam Lewis Walker is the go-to man. Not only has he lived an elite life, he has interviewed hundreds of other elite men about what it takes to reach your maximum potential. The results are in this book. Adam represents this space with humility, grace and tons of energy. Best part is Adam the person is as good as it gets. He simply makes everyone around him better.'

TIM DIXON
Elite performance coach and author of *The Mental Locker*

'*Awaken Your Alpha* was just brilliant. I found it an inspiring and compelling read, and hard to put down! I would highly recommend this real-world guidebook as a "must have" for anyone interested in achieving their true potential.'

RAMY ROMANY
Multiple Emmy-award-winning cinematographer and director

'In this book, Adam has assisted me in awakening my "inner man". This comes from a sense of self-awareness, a built-in resilience and solemn promise to ourselves that no matter how many times we get knocked down, what counts is how many times we get back up.

'The truth is that *every* man is going through his own set of challenges. We are meant to toil away, bring home the bacon, go through the stress of work and business, and somehow still have a smile on our face at the end of the day. Society and the male ego have forced us to become competitive with the outside world. In reality, our biggest competition is with ourselves. This book has provided me with great insight and tools for how to become the best version of myself.'

ALPESH H PATEL
Founder of Mi-Fone and author of *Tested*

'Over the course of this book, Adam shares insightful, powerful and – most importantly – actionable mindsets and principles you can use to improve your life across many different domains. He illustrates the principles with profound stories from his own life as well as [those of] other thought-leaders, experts and high performers. No matter where you're currently at, there is a nugget of wisdom contained in these pages that will help you get to the next level of achievement.'

RYAN BLACK
Executive dating coach and co-founder of Infinite Man Summit

'What does it mean to be a man? A real man in today's world. It's not easy and it's only going to get tougher. In *Awaken Your Alpha*, Adam Lewis Walker has created the road map for a man of any age. He gives us a step by step process to quickly become the man we really want to be. I'm delighted about this as the world needs more real men.'

DAVID SHEPHARD
NLP master trainer and founder of The Performance Partnership

'This book provides many methods and paths to accelerate your success in life. Delivered through the stories of dozens of high achievers with Adam's expert insight and ideas. Thankfully he has done the hard work.'

KAVIT HARIA

Online business strategist and author of *Don't Sleep On It!*

'It's times like this that we need a new way forward for the men of this world. This is where Adam's book comes in. It is a must read for every man that wants to step up in their life with confidence and a vision of being a conscious leader.'

TOM CRONIN

Meditation master and founder of The Stillness Project

'*Awaken Your Alpha* outlines an effective model to help you identify, isolate, and address the differences between the man you are and the one you want to be. In addition to highlighting a bevy of men from around the world and their approach to overcoming adversity, Adam asks the hard questions needed to push through limiting beliefs with tactics that actually "move the needle" in your life.'

JOHN ROMANIELLO

Fitness Expert and NYT Best-selling Author *Engineering The Alpha*

CONTENTS

ACT II: ACTION

ACT III: ASCENSION

CLOSING ACT

To my sons Dylan and Harrison,
who one day will be men

PREFACE

'One's own free, untrammeled desires,
one's own whim... all of this is precisely that which fits
no classification, and which is constantly knocking all
systems and theories to hell. And where did our sages
get the idea that man must have normal, virtuous
desires? What man needs is only his own independent
wishing, whatever that independence may
cost and wherever it may lead.'

FYODOR DOSTOYEVSKY

TODAY IS INDEPENDENCE DAY

'How do I start?' This is the thought bouncing around my head this morning as I wander outside to see the sun reflecting off a beautiful and nearly perfectly flat lake. All I intend to do is get out on the paddle board – not thinking about how I will do it, but walking forward boldly into action.

Action: just start; work out the details later.

As it turns out, both my boys have woken up, like the sound of my idea and jump on board, too. They are a little tribe I have attracted through my action, definiteness of purpose, and ultimately, my fun mission. An adventure.

This is life.

The answer to my question at the top of this chapter comes to me as we approach the middle of the lake, heading to explore the island. Talking to the boys, I can't believe we are not on holiday; that we live here. And it strikes me: how can I not write this book?

This is my first Independence Day since I moved to the United States from England. A day celebrating independence and freedom. This experience, this life is what I was yearning for, but I couldn't quite place my finger on it five years ago. It's what every 'alpha' needs – your own personal freedom and independence; to create and lead a life you love to live and have an impact; to be a positive example for your children, as they will be your legacy. They will not just follow your words, but how you choose to live your life today and every day.

Many people are comfortable going through the motions in life, accepting the current set up regardless of their level of happiness. That's their free choice. This book is not for them. This book is for those who, like me, choose an alternative path; who have a desire to do more, be more, love more, and are in pursuit of continual improvement.

Four years ago, when I was back in England in what turned out to be my last job, the life I have now was all just a dream. What made this dream different to all my other dreams was that it had a sense of urgency about it. I was fed up with it just being a dream, so it became a personal ultimatum.

If not now, when?

I decided now. I went against advice and quit my job.

You have to have a plan B, right? A solid back-up? Well, I did. As a qualified teacher, I was never going to go hungry. There is always work for a decent teacher. My back would never be against the wall, so if things didn't work out, never mind. I would not be marooned on an island where I would have to fight to survive. I was comfortable – and this was what was slowly killing me.

In quitting teaching, I removed my plan B and burned my bridges so there was no going back. That decision, followed up with constant action, is why I am about to write this book, sharing what I learn every day from others with a similar drive. My continued journey is within these pages. I could write ten books from my research and interviews, but could is worthless. I must start with one book, one page, one word – dive in and not hold back. In twelve months, I'll be a different guy.

I will only include what I have found helpful, both inspirationally and practically. It is my intention that you too will be inspired to have a positive impact on the world. If you take away just one thing from this book, implement it and have a result that improves your quality of life. Then in my mind, job done.

I knew it was a great idea to write this book.

Adam Lewis Walker

Grand Lake, Northern Michigan, USA
Independence Day, 10.52 am, Tuesday 4 July 2017

INTRODUCTION

'Man goes to great trouble to acquire
knowledge of the material world.
He learns all branches of mundane science.
He explores the earth, and even
travels to the moon. Yet he never tries to
find out what exists within himself.
Because he is unaware of the enormous
power which lies hidden within him.'

ANONYMOUS, ANCIENT HINDU TEXT

POLE VAULTING IN THE RAIN

Growing up, I was obsessed by sport. I loved the Olympics and the ideal behind it (Olympism is a philosophy of life, combining as a balanced whole the qualities of body, will and mind), and it definitely shaped my life choices.

Fast forward to 3pm on 3 August 2008, an Olympic year. It was the UK Challenge Final at Windsor and I was competing in the men's pole vault. It had taken me twenty-eight years to get here and it was my biggest competition to date. The weather was classic of the English summertime: horizontal rain.

There were four competitors left and I was sitting in fourth place. The conditions were getting worse, the track was flooded, and only our spikes kept us from slipping, but I was thinking about one thing: getting a medal. With the bar being raised, I needed to do something different.

I reached for my larger vaulting pole – the one that I only used in great conditions. I ran down towards the vault, feeling determined, but at the last second, I ran through as it hadn't felt right. Angry with myself, I walked back for my second attempt and heard a voice from the crowd.

'He's done, he won't take off again.'

I remember thinking that no matter what, I *would* get off the ground this time. I had lost perspective. I came in fast, I got close. It felt wrong again, but I went for it. My heel hit the ground first and I slipped on take-off...

Dislocated kneecap, torn cruciate ligament (ACL), meniscus cartilage torn to shreds, and bruised bone ends from the impact. The pain was immense.

That one moment changed everything. Initially I was upbeat (generally I am), but I think I was in shock for some time. About a year into what turned out to be two years of crutches, multiple operations, rehab and the realisation I would never compete again, I was not OK. I used to be a pole-vaulter; I didn't know what I was now. My whole identity had gone, and I was lost.

If you have ever felt truly lost, you will know what I am talking about. If you haven't, it's likely you will experience it at some point. I became depressed, I was ashamed of how I felt, and that intensified the downward spiral. The lowest point came when my mum called me in the middle of the day, asking if I was OK. I said I was, but I wasn't. We hung up, and I cried uncontrollably for no clear reason. I couldn't stop.

From the tone in my voice, my mum must have known I was far from OK because she turned up on my doorstep. I was a broken man. I felt powerless. I had quit my teaching job just before the accident to launch a business where I needed to be active, and now I had to start again; to reinvent; to awaken something inside of me. Each day, I had to battle for my alpha. It was not easy, but lives that are easy are boring and uninspiring.

'This is the true athlete – the person in rigorous training against false impressions. Remain firm, you who suffer, don't be kidnapped by your impressions! The struggle is great, the task divine – to gain mastery, freedom, happiness and tranquillity.'

EPICTETUS, GREEK STOIC PHILOSOPHER, BORN A SLAVE

I believe each man can achieve greatness and happiness at the same time. I know now this is achieved in the moment you decide to act on living to your true potential. Blaming, complaining and hoping will not make it happen. Awareness and action will.

Robert Greene, the bestselling Author of *Mastery*, argues we all have the ability to push the limits of human potential. We have access to information that past masters could only dream about. That is why I believe the power comes in your application. Conditions are never perfect, so now is the 'perfect' time to begin.

THE DEFINITION OF ALPHA

Society and the media can sometimes view the alpha male negatively. The true meaning has been distorted over the years to a knuckle-dragging, aggressive meathead 'bully boy'. The world's view of a man would have us believe we must finish school, put our heads down and work flat out for life to achieve monetary success. Whether we like the work or it brings any good to the world is irrelevant. Have a wife, children, a home, fancy cars – lots of stuff to show off our level of manliness.

The issue is, if you go down this road, you may wake up eventually and realise you have missed out on what is really important. Your kids will be grown, you may have drifted away from your partner, and most likely die a few short years after you stop the job that you prioritised over everything.

This is not the 'alpha' I am referring to. The definition from the animal kingdom is: 'Having the highest rank in a dominance hierarchy, eg the alpha of an elephant pack'. The definition from the Solar System is: 'The brightest star in a constellation, eg Alpha Centauri'. I want to shift the focus back to these origins: the highest rank; the brightest star.

For centuries, successful people have known how to awaken their alpha, or whatever they called it at the time. They have known the mindset and strategies to win at life. With varying commitment, we all pursue this wisdom today. To me, the concept of *Awaken Your Alpha* is the personal pursuit to shine as brightly as you can with your time on this earth; to achieve the highest rank in what you hold important in your life; to be:

- The best father, the best son
- The best husband or partner
- In the best health, mental and physical
- Wealthy, and not just in terms of money
- The best friend and have the best friendships
- Using your unique talents to the best of your ability
- Making the best use of your time

This is a lifestyle that knows no division of nationality, race, gender, religion or sexuality; it is open to all who choose to pursue it. It comes from a position of abundance, not scarcity. Your highest rank is not something to be judged by others or a prize that you've won. Shining brightly is not to put others into your shadow, but to light them up.

We all have limitless possibilities to create our life: the difference is being aware that it is a choice, and then having the belief in ourselves to start living that choice. The key to high performance is to *Awaken Your Alpha* each and every day.

I have collaborated with, coached and interviewed hundreds of men specifically on the subject of 'How to *Awaken Your Alpha*', breaking my findings down into three essential phases which form the foundation of the book:

Awareness – Action – Ascension

This is how other men have overcome adversity to rise up, and how you can too. The strength to *Awaken Your Alpha* is within you; it is within all of us. Most are able to do it sporadically, but the power comes with consistency where this state becomes your norm; where you sit with inner strength and your true self on a daily basis. By unlocking and accessing your alpha to the highest level possible, you cannot fail to benefit.

Throughout the book, I will guide you to operate from a position of inner power and confidence to impact your view of what you can achieve, both physically and mentally. Having interviewed more than 200 of the world's alpha minds over the four years I spent researching this book, I have noticed many methods and messages being repeated by different guests. There is an overlap between the three sections of the book, but no man can create the life he is truly capable of without understanding and applying all three sections. There is no putting a man into one clear box.

Success leaves clues, so I have picked out the best and most inspiring examples to me, putting them in appropriate places to illustrate a point or principle you can apply in your life. There are many essential fundamentals to excelling here, but beyond that,

I have avoided a one-size-fits-all approach. I can't just say 'Take more risks' or 'Work harder'. Some of you reading this need to take more risks and get to work, while others will need to take fewer risks and do less work before you break down. I believe most men are already too harsh on themselves, but you may be too self-forgiving.

I see too many cult-like men's groups, always in warrior mode that leaves little space for individuality. With this book, the accompanying podcast and my coaching, I aim to build solid foundations to improve our own judgements on all our life decisions. Focus in on what you must take from this book to move forward. As a coach, I know this is where the power of individual attention and accountability comes into its own.

The formula I have created and used as a framework for this book is by no means a finished know-all system. As I follow the *Kaizen* path (*kaizen* is the Japanese word for 'continual improvement' or 'change for better'), how could it be? It is, however, a clear process; a working document. I want you to work with this book, make notes and do the exercises – use it to have an impact.

> 'Life without design is erratic. As soon
> as one is in place, principles become necessary.
> I think you'll concede that nothing is more shameful
> than uncertain and wavering conduct, and beating a
> cowardly retreat. This will happen in all our affairs
> unless we remove the faults that seize and detain
> our spirits, preventing them from pushing
> forward and making an all-out effort.'
>
> **SENECA, ROMAN STOIC PHILOSOPHER**

QUALITY OF YOUR LIFE

Quality of your life = quality of your questions.

Throughout the book there are thirty-one boxes with questions and actions to make this a more impactful experience. Depending on how you roll, you can complete them in your own journal or reach out to grab the accompanying resources from www.ayalpha.com – whatever works better for you.

The boxes for 'action' are:

1. Your reality
2. Your vision
3. Cross the gap
4. Mission
5. Priority actions
6. Motto
7. Checklists don't lie
8. Your code, your call
9. Pomodoro
10. I expect
11. The tripod
12. Premeditation of evils
13. Actionable
14. A better way?
15. The Dickens process
16. A positive alternative
17. Hunt or hold
18. Energy current
19. Money tripod
20. Dough diagnosis
21. Money mode
22. Recovery
23. Align
24. Incident–point–benefit
25. Moment in the zone
26. Toxic list
27. The 11th law
28. Experience
29. Respect
30. Ikigai
31. You're dead

The more tough conversations we are willing to have (including with ourselves), the more we will improve our lives. If you never ask or work to answer your tough questions, life will be harder than it has to be. I am reminded of this when I find myself burying my head in the sand, which is always swiftly followed by the quality of my life dropping off.

'Life shrinks or expands in proportion to one's courage.'

ANAÏS NIN, AUTHOR OF *IN FAVOR OF THE SENSITIVE MAN*

THE ULTIMATUM

What are you looking to get out of this book?

There is a reason you have this in your hands today. It could have been anyone else reading this, but it's not. It is you choosing to read this.

Everyone will get something different from the book, depending on what they are looking for. As with life itself, having that awareness early will make it a better experience for you. In your life story every day, a page is turning, and you are the one holding the pen. You alone decide whether it will be a bestseller or put you straight to sleep, but you don't get a rewrite. From this point onwards, you can make sure your life story has a strong finish.

Let's crack on.

ACT I

AWARENESS

'Each man and woman has consummate
inner genius within them. It's their awareness or
unawareness of this inner genius that determines
their ability to make themselves a
master or stay mediocre.'

WALTER RUSSELL, AUTHOR OF *THE UNIVERSAL ONE*

I will be breaking 'Awareness' down into

PURPOSE
PRIORITIES
PROCESS
PERSPECTIVE

In this section you will:

- Gain clarity on who you are, and why you are where you are now
- Identify the man you want to become, and what you must do now as a priority
- Develop your personal philosophy and code
- Understand the impact of your mission (even if you have not yet clarified it – which is OK)
- Decide on specific daily actions that will move you forward as a man

PURPOSE

'What is the point of being alive if you don't
at least try to do something remarkable?'

JOHN GREEN, AUTHOR OF *THE FAULT IN OUR STARS*

A famous and overused quote tells us that the mass of men lead lives of quiet desperation, which I believe is true. Worse still, the impact of a man leading a life of desperation is not limited to him as an individual. The additional impact on his loved ones, women, men and children, is huge.

This is why I wish to share tales and tactics to thrive as a man. You've got to have a positive impact in your life and in the lives of those around you. As I have already mentioned, this book has found itself into your hands for a reason. Let's work out why together.

You have to know who you are. As Robert Greene, bestselling author of *The 48 Laws of Power*, put it in our interview:

'If you're just simply on social media all the time, have no idea of what makes you different and an individual, what your source of power is, what your uniqueness is… your primal inclinations and what you were meant to do in life. If you have no knowledge of that, forget it. You'll never get anywhere. You'll try different jobs. They won't work, you'll be bitter, resentful and you'll be terrible at the power game.'

The key is to have awareness about yourself. Do you know what you want? Do you know what you're good at?

ARE YOU SURE?

All men have basic needs and drives: the need for significance, connection, love, growth and contribution. In addition, we have a need for certainty, but also a need for uncertainty.

The level of certainty you need, which is different for all men, goes a long way towards explaining your personal happiness. It's why men can be inspired or desperate in seemingly similar circumstances. As a schoolteacher, I felt the level of certainty was too high. Consistent pay cheque, similar lessons and confined curriculum meant too much predictability. The lack of long-term potential to grow stressed me out; lack of growth is ultimately death to an alpha. In this environment, I knew I would have spent too much time operating out of desperation instead of inspiration, and I was not willing to accept that.

Where do you fit on the continuums for different aspects of your life? Your needs can be similar or different depending on the aspect of your life – for example, you may want an element of uncertainty in your work, but not in your partner. If you were to draw a line from certainty to uncertainty, marking where your current reality and your ideal scenario are for each aspect of your life, would they be close or in conflict? If the two marks match up, that's legendary. There is a great chance you are one happy dude, or at least on the right path for you. If they are poles apart, then it's likely you are one pissed-off and frustrated guy.

With that in mind, assess who and where are you *now*. Not your past, not your future, but the current reality of you. Examine the role you are playing in this world.

Self-observation is essential for self-growth. You need to be brutality honest and accurate with yourself. Don't sugar coat it; it is what it is. Everyone and anyone can make up reasons or statistics to warp the truth, but unless you're planning on running for President, you don't need to do that. Stick to the truth.

ACTION 1: YOUR REALITY (POINT A)

In each of these seven key areas: spiritual/mentality, physical/ energy, intimate partner, family, friends, community and business/work, rank your personal satisfaction out of ten, with zero being awful and ten being legendary. Remember, this is your *current* satisfaction. Add all your scores and divide the result by seven to get your overall current life satisfaction.

This is a simple way to track who you believe you are now, and a great exercise to repeat at least every three months to see where your focus is most needed. Your lowest scoring two to three areas are always good places to start. What would you have to do to increase their scores by a point or two in the next three months?

Next, find your vision. Where do you want to go and who do you want to become?

> 'One day, Alice came to a fork in the road and saw a Cheshire cat in a tree. "Which road do I take?" she asked. "Where do you want to go?" was his response. "I don't know," Alice answered. "Then," said the cat, "it doesn't matter."'
>
> **LEWIS CARROLL, *ALICE IN WONDERLAND***

If you have no vision, no mission, you will be similar to Alice, stuck in your own Wonderland. Unfortunately, it probably will not be too wonderful. I personally struggle when my mission becomes unclear, as I'm more likely to become a victim of circumstance.

Your vision is just that: *your* vision. You need to have one to guide you. If you struggle with finding your vision, often being aware of what you don't like and don't want can head you in the right direction to discover what you do want.

MOUNT OLYMPUS

ACTION 2: YOUR VISION (POINT B)

- What does your ideal alpha life look like?
- What do you want to achieve?
- What are you good at and could be great at?
- What are you motivated about doing?
- What feels easy to you, but others find difficult?
- What do you want?
- What would your days and weeks look like if you had it?

Write your answers down in as much descriptive detail as possible. What would you be doing in your ideal alpha life? Who would you be around? Where would you be and why? What will you need to have achieved in one year from now to be on track, if it is not your vision to be at point B in one year?

Revisit your statement and add to it as you go through the book. Your vision may not be clear yet.

When you have the awareness of where you are today and where you want to be tomorrow, you have a set point A and point B. More importantly, if you have been honest, you are now aware of the size of the gap between the two points, big or small. Awareness of this gap is a powerful step.

Finally, you need to claim this gap; it's yours and no one else's. What did you do to get to point A and what do you need to do to get to point B?

Claiming your life means taking responsibility to find the answers to all its challenges, not focusing on others to make this happen or waiting for people to 'discover' you. We can get very good at explaining why something hasn't happened or blaming others because we are not where we want to be. Just stop. This is the playing field of your life. Blaming others is much like sport players focusing on the umpire or referee when they don't get the result they are after. Truly accept you have a role to play in everything, big or small.

Brian Tracy, who is the most listened-to Audio Author on personal and business success in the world today, told me a story about a traveller in ancient Greece. The traveller met an old man walking along the road and asked him how to get to Mount Olympus. The old man, who turned out to be Socrates, turned and pointed at the mountain summit in the distance.

'Just make sure every step you take is in that direction.'

Simple, but powerful. This is where life becomes exciting: an adventure where you claim and take responsibility for your mission. Every step you take, you are either walking towards your summit – your point B, your vision – or away from it. You cannot stay still.

ACTION 3: CROSS THE GAP

Split a piece of paper or a page in your journal in two with a line down the middle. On one side, list the activities that got you to point A, keep you where you currently are, and don't allow your growth (negative). On the other side, list the activities that will get you to point B (where you want to go). Have a 'tactics dump' with practical things to do that will better you, helping you progress and grow.

Make sure to include daily, weekly and monthly actions for both. We'll come back to them later... *mwhahahaha.*

MAN ON A MISSION

JAMES G. BUTLER, USA

> 'You will become as small as your controlling desire; as great as your dominant aspiration.'
>
> **JAMES ALLEN, AUTHOR OF *AS A MAN THINKETH***

James was a former military diver, Afghanistan veteran, bomb disposal expert, and men's transformational coach. During our interview in 2017, we talked specifically about men and their mission.

This was the only interview during which I told the guest, 'This is definitely going in the book.' During the book's writing process, James's podcast interview was released, and we spoke at length one more time about our missions, catching up and deciding how we could collaborate in the future.

About a month later, as I finished the first draft, I caught the news. While swimming off Thailand with his fiancée, James had dived down and never came back up. He died unexpectedly at just twenty-eight years of age, before he had the chance to see his story published.

During the interview, James kept coming back to the subject of choosing his path in life. Even when his mission wasn't clear, he was certain a life of significance was his priority, whatever the risk. This was how he found himself as an elite bomb disposal expert.

During his bomb disposal years, James formed a positive relationship with adversity. As men, we all have the chance to rise to challenges, strengthen our will and find a way. It may not be as extreme as James's, but without any challenges, we will sink to our situation and below. On the flip side, as James described, the more adverse a situation becomes, the more extraordinary we can become. We have to.

James recalled a situation in Afghanistan, which I have included as an example of the extraordinary things we men are capable of, both good and bad, when the incentive is there (your life). James's role on patrol was to be the front guy. Every first step taken was his; every wall to be jumped, he jumped.

'Our patrol had broken up into two groups and we were coming up behind them, going to target. I jumped over a wall, looked up and one of the guys in the other patrol just explodes. At the moment, dust is falling, ears ringing. It's like slow motion for a lot of that time.

'So, you can imagine, someone just passed away and the people that put that [explosive] in the ground were then shooting at us. I had to move a distance from where I was to where the patrol were, knowing if there was going to be anything in the ground, I had to find it. Keep in mind you've grown to love every single man that you're with. It's a lot coming at you at one place, at that time. Full responsibility: I'm both responsible for keeping myself alive and now I'm responsible for keeping them alive.'

James was twenty-one at the time. He explained that when an explosive device goes off, there's metal everywhere, so you can't just use a metal detector.

'You take a knife and you poke the ground in a 45-degree angle and hope that you hit it from the side instead of hitting it from the top. You go inch by inch and it's 58 degrees Celsius.'

He went on to discover six devices in the ground that day, one of them only inches from his friend's foot.

'If he had just turned around, that would have been it.' Perspective comes in here.

'I've never felt so weak in my entire life. Then in another second, you go, "Well if I can go through that, there's nothing I can't go through." There's nothing you can't be.'

This is the power of a clear mission, even when you're facing extreme challenges.

James was hooked and made it his mission to advance to a more elite unit: deep-sea bomb disposal. After about three years of spending all his waking moments practising to be an elite-performing human, he got into the unit.

Forty days in, he had a failure of his left lung and woke up in hospital eight days later. James went from being at the peak of his fitness to waking up 65 pounds lighter, unable to walk, let alone fulfil his purpose, his mission. Everything changed.

Identity for all men is hugely important. Regardless of your environment or situation, if you identify with something and you've got a mission, you can perform miracles. You can strive every day to move forward.

When you lose your identity or mission, you are lost as a man. There will be times in your life you will feel this way more than others – I felt most lost after my accident ruined my athletics career. When you know how well you can perform, what you can accomplish, it's tough to take when you are in limbo.

As James put it:

> 'I know how much courage I have. I know that I can go from zero to a hundred and I can train to do anything I need to do. Suddenly I have nowhere to put any of that.'

Ultimately, the issue is the pain of not having a mission any longer. We have all of these powers in our lives: we've got time, we've got money, relationships, and we've got resources, but often, we use them in sporadic ways with no notable or common focus. The hardest part is trying to pin your focus down to 'What the hell do I want to do?'

If you feel like you are underperforming, not putting it out there to the level you know you can achieve, you're not going to be fulfilled. It's not a good place to be in. Once you begin to move in the right direction, it's a lot easier to harness your power.

ACTION 4: MISSION

I asked you earlier about your vision, your ideal life in detail. Now I am asking, 'What is your mission?' Not what can you do, but what is your mission within your vision?

You can do anything, so what do you want to do? If you don't know, that is fine, so long as you are aware of the fact. Leaving the answer blank is a key marker. Make the decision to find your mission. Use some of the ideas below to help.

THE HERO'S JOURNEY

What are you afraid your mission actually is? What is so big that you're afraid it's too big?

A lot of times, when we think about our missions, we're coming from a disempowered place. We're thinking from fear; we're coming from survival instincts. So, when we think about what we want to do or be, the foundation isn't firm enough to build anything of value or excitement.

It is a common mistake to take the approach of 'I'm going to do the *thing*, and once I achieve the *thing*, that will make me feel like the man I want to be'. I believe we must first be the man we want to be, so then we can do the thing we want to do. Everything in your life has been uniquely designed to make you the hero of your story.

'By actually having lived through adversity, you've learned this "thing" and this is why you are whole. It's why you're complete and perfect for the journey ahead right now; you're ready to go, man. What you don't have is OK, and you'll get that along the way. You will always grow, but as you are right now, you are perfect.

'Let's get to that firm foundation of powerful, capable and free so people can go, "Ahhhhhh, even if I don't have my mission yet, I'm good."'

Now when we're looking for that 'thing', that mission, as the man we are meant to be, it becomes a lot easier because everything is open to us. First the relationship with ourselves begins to appear, then the mission, and we start to question, what would make an impact?

'What if you actually did it? Would it move you to tears waking up in the middle of the night? If you didn't need to make money, if you had all the money in the world, [what is it] that you would still just do?'

In order to get into that conversation, you really have to be on a firm foundation. Do not create a mission out of desperation, but out of inspiration – it makes a massive difference. If it is out of desperation, the desperation will come through in all you do, and that's no fun at all.

The journey part of every man's mission is about understanding how to be in unknown circumstances, how to behave when the odds are not in your favour, knowing that you can say yes to something you have no clue how to do. On the way, you will become the person you need to be. Do not choose missions or goals that you're capable of doing right now; choose something that you will have to become a different person to achieve. That is where breakthroughs happen.

When you take on something that you cannot do right now, you have the chance to become the man who is capable of accomplishing it. You have the chance to grow. You'll have to think and do things differently to develop in a different way, because the challenge is bigger than you (for now).

PRIORITIES

'The key is not to prioritize what's on
your schedule, but to schedule your priorities.'

DR STEPHEN COVEY, AUTHOR OF *THE 7 HABITS OF HIGHLY EFFECTIVE PEOPLE*

NOTHING IS HARDER TO LEARN

T he importance of pursuing and discovering your true role in
this world is huge. Being just a little off on this can be the
difference between being good and being legendary. Not being
aware of its importance at all is a sure-fire way to struggle in life.

So, what are your priorities right now? You must have a solid foundation
first, fix the leaks, and get into the right head space. To improve your
life, what needs attention now and in the next month?

ACTION 5: PRIORITY ACTIONS

Write down the three areas which rated lowest in the 'your reality'
exercise. Now pick the one that feels most urgent to you. Look at
all the tactics you listed for that and add more now if needed.

Out of that, pick the top one to three practical tactics that
will have an impact on your score. Include daily, weekly and
monthly actions.

Repeat this process for one or two more areas that received
your lowest ratings. These are your three focuses (maximum)
with practical, actionable tactics to improve.

If you do your priority actions consistently, it will have a positive impact. Everything else is just fluff. Once you have clarified your priorities, be ruthless with your execution – I'll cover how to track this in the 'Process' section of the book. Sure, you can do additional stuff, but not at the expense of the priorities you have identified.

The small decisions we make daily make our lives, simple as that. Only we can decide figuratively whether to 'Put the cookie down!' (the first, but not the last, Arnold quote you will see in the book). In all seriousness, if you did decide, consciously or unconsciously, to eat cookies multiple times a day, every day, year after year, for example, you would be a mess in the long term.

If you say, 'I should do this', you are already declaring it isn't going to happen. Committing means turning a 'should' into a 'must'. You create the life you *must* live, not the one you *should*. 'Shoulds' do not get done, 'musts' do.

Who must you become to achieve what you want?

'There is nothing the busy man is less busied
with than living; there is nothing harder to learn.'

SENECA, ROMAN STOIC PHILOSOPHER

BE RELENTLESS

TRAVIS JONES, AUSTRALIA

Travis is a blunt, to-the-point Aussie, and his was the most downloaded podcast during the first year of *Awaken Your Alpha*. To do his words justice, you really need to hear him speak them aloud.

Travis is the man behind the Results Based Training gym empire. Originally, he worked his way up through Fitness First as a trainer.

> 'I had my own business, but it's more like a really shitty job because you have to pay them [Fitness First], and you work all the time. I became a manager of four clubs for them. I hated authority. I was like, "That's it, I'm opening up a gym." So, I get myself a six-week arena to open the gym.

> 'I got a location; it fell through two weeks before I was to open. I found another location in three days, which was twice the price, and I was like, "Fuck it, I'm going to do it." I think it is when you have the will so big that you know nothing is going to stop you. It's the twenty-two-hour days that feel like only four-hour days because you love it so much.'

Most of us know the flip side: if you're doing crappy work that you're just competent in, a six-hour day can feel like twenty hours.

Travis had to live upstairs in his gym with his dog. He didn't have enough money to pay the AU$12,000 a month rent. Groupon deals were getting big at the time, so he decided to do a sauna deal. He had twelve days left until he would be kicked out, only three months into getting his dream off the ground.

Travis launched the deal, and within seven days had sold AU$15,000 worth of sauna deals. He just needed to take care of one minor detail now.

'I called up a sauna company: "I need a sauna quick, delivered to my gym." I essentially got a sauna for free, had AU$1,000 in my pocket and survived for another month. I actually haven't really told anyone this: I couldn't make rent the next month either.

'I went to a guy I knew had some money, said, "Give me AU$10k and I'll give you AU$20k back in twelve weeks." I contacted a lawyer to put it together, signed it and he gave me the money. I was seeing at a level that nothing was going to stop me.'

In his own words, Travis didn't have the most talent, but he did possess a relentless work ethic to make his vision a reality, no matter what. There are parallels to what Will Smith has said about his own attitude to work.

'I will not be out-worked, period. You might have more talent than me, you might be smarter than me, you might be sexier than me, you might be all of those things… but if we get on the treadmill together, there's two things: you're getting off first, or I'm going to die.'

CANNIBALISE YOUR DREAMS

Like Travis, I believe there are times we all need to draw our line in the sand, where we'll do anything within our moral code to succeed. To do this, we need to make sure our vision is so inspiring that we are willing to commit and make ourselves succeed.

Nine months later, Travis was making the equivalent of half a million dollars a year. What I find significant is he had no plan B. Robert Greene, the bestselling author of *The 48 Laws of Power*, calls this the 'death grab', which I will cover in more detail in the 'Achieve' chapter. It's all about the level of commitment, and that was a big weakness for me.

I always had a pretty cushy plan B as a teacher. If my 'thing' didn't go that well, plan B was still good enough. In the end, I had to forcibly remove my nice plan B because I realised it was holding me back from fully committing.

To a point, a back-up is good, but sometimes, you need the hunger of 'it must work' to commit fully. If you always have a plan B, it can cannibalise your dreams.

THE PUSSIFICATION OF MAN

If you're sitting on the fence concerning commitment, you'll achieve nothing apart from getting splinters up your arse. You need to hear this message from the 'softly spoken' Travis.

> 'When people say they can't afford to know, to understand what they need to do, buy a fucking book... It's not you can't afford to do it, you're just fucking lazy. So, Awaken Your Alpha and get the fuck off your bed. You have a passion, you have something you can give back, and you're holding it to yourself, so you're fucking sabotaging the rest of the universe. You can change more lives than just yourself. Try to help five people a week, because if you're not helping people, you're a bit of a dick. That's the truth.

> 'Look, guys, if you're hearing this, stop being a fucking pussy. Stop the pussification of mankind. Stop wearing such tight jeans that squash your balls. Go for a run, lift some heavy shit, do things that scare you, help someone out and learn

something daily. The race of males is becoming a scared race of individuals. If you're not learning, you're losing. If you don't do this stuff, you're going to end up being an "I coulda, I woulda, I shoulda"... You're going to look back in three years, nothing's going to change, and you're going to say, "Bad luck hit me." It's not fucking bad luck.'

'The only person you are destined to become is the person you decide to be.'

RALPH WALDO EMERSON, AMERICAN TRANSCENDENTALIST POET

PROCESS

'The warrior who trusts his path
doesn't need to prove the other is wrong.'

PAULO COELHO, AUTHOR OF *THE ALCHEMIST*

Truly experience the phase and the moment you are in. When you have decided you will accomplish great things in this life, and what the great things are, trust the process and stay the course.

You may create intentional imbalance as part of your process. Intentional imbalance is a term I first heard in the bestselling book *The 12 Week Year* by Brian P. Moran and Michael Lennington. The basic concept is that trying to spend equal time in each area of your life to achieve 'life balance' can be frustrating, unproductive and unfulfilling as a life choice. At different times in your life, you will choose to focus on one area over another, and that's OK. In fact, it can be a powerful move. The key is it has to be intentional and in line with your priorities. This is how you will be able to deal with the biggest priority you have identified and give it the extra energy it needs before your life becomes unsustainable.

With intentional imbalance (which is usually short term), it is critical to get back to your balance swiftly as part of your process. On the most basic level, if I am going to be away for an event, I ensure I have extra family days beforehand, afterwards or both to address my intentional imbalance. It's an easy process to apply, but it's also easy not to do. Make your own agreements around intentional imbalance and don't let yourself or others down.

'NEVER COMPLAIN, NEVER EXPLAIN'

This is a quote from Benjamin Disraeli, a British prime minister from the nineteenth century, and was given to me by author Robert Greene as his favourite quote.

'Basically, just don't complain in life. People don't like to hear it. There's nothing to complain about because your life is what it should be; it's what you get from it.

'Don't explain yourself. Don't sit there and waste words, "Oh, I meant to do this" or "You should hear me, this is what I'm good at." Just fucking do it and let your deeds speak for themselves. I love that. It's like four words to explain my philosophy.'

I ask the same question to every guest who comes on the *Awaken Your Alpha* podcast: 'What is a quote that resonates with you, that you like to live your life by?' I love quotes, as I am sure you are beginning to notice, but that is not why I ask the question. I ask it to understand each person's approach to life and their basic philosophy. We all have one, whether we are aware of it or not. Think of Richard Branson's famous *Screw It, Let's Do It* book. If you look at his past and present adventures, I'd say this title rings true as a life philosophy.

What is yours? Mine can be summed up pretty well by combining these quotes: 'Do it, do it now' from the movie *Predator* (my favourite movie), which I have painted across a whole wall in my office. 'Life shrinks or expands in proportion to one's courage', Anaïs Nin, and 'Success is never final' from former British Prime Minister Winston Churchill. Your intention should be to step into action now in spite of fear; you can't just 'do it' and then stop. It is a continual application of yourself daily, not some destination to hit. This helps me take bolder action, be more present and enjoy the journey, as that is all I will ever have.

ACTION 6: MOTTO

What are your favourite quotes? What really resonates with you and your approach to life? Think about it and write them down.

Make your quotes into your own motto, and change what you need to achieve it.

Understand, clarify and embrace your 'motto'. Yes, you can just work on your attitude, actions and ultimately your achievements, but over time, they will align with your personal philosophy (motto). This personal philosophy creates your attitude, your attitude creates your habits, and your habits create your results. These results create your life.

If we take the time to think and plan, many of us know what we need to do. It is in the consistent discipline to do the work of executing our priorities where we lose the way. This is where the power of accountability makes the difference. At the very least, hold yourself accountable. Track your own execution ruthlessly without making excuses.

This is where a coach becomes an invaluable tactic of the world's high-achieving men.

ACTION 7: CHECKLISTS DON'T LIE

Create a simple checklist for only the priority actions you identified earlier. Include daily, weekly and monthly tactics. Your daily tactic could be for every day or just specific days; you decide. Just tick it off every day/time you complete it.

For example, with a seven-day tactic, if at the end of the week you have ticked it seven times, you have executed at it at 100%. If you ticked it four times, you have executed it at just over 60%.

If your planning is right, you will achieve what you set out to do at 100% execution, or likely even 90% consistently. Below 80% execution and you will not.

AGREEMENTS TO SIMPLIFY LIFE

By making and keeping a code, a set of vital agreements that you live by, you'll become known as a man who keeps his word and is worth trusting. One of my favourite approaches is simplicity + discipline = freedom. To the average man, discipline and rules are not associated with freedom. This is a key mistake.

In my interview with Craig Ballantyne (Craig has been called the world's most disciplined man), the author of *The Perfect Day Formula*, he touched on this distinction.

'It is tempting to go with the crowd and stay up late each night, watching television or drinking too much alcohol, and sleep late the next morning. That is the way of the average man and gets us nothing but average results in a world where average has become unacceptable, unbearable and unrewarding.'

It would be easy for me to list my code and my rules, but I want to focus on creating your own code and rules – what you will and won't tolerate. What you are and are not willing to sacrifice to progress. This way, any situation you find yourself in and any decision you need to make will become simpler. You can review the options within your chosen code, asking yourself, 'Will this move me a step towards my Mount Olympus or further away?'

ACTION 8: YOUR CODE, YOUR CALL

Let's get you going with some basic themes to create your code around. These ideas are not exclusive or all-inclusive.

- Bedtime
- Wake-up time
- Diet
- Caffeine intake
- Alcohol intake
- Exercise
- Morning routine
- Evening routine
- Email/phone time
- In-person communication
- Writing/journaling
- Mission
- To-do lists and not-to-do lists
- Fun/excitement
- Health
- Family

Below are two basic rules from Craig Ballantyne and two from me to show the adjustment you need for your individual ownership.

Craig's rule: I will go to bed at 8pm and get up at 4am seven days a week.

My rule: I will go to bed no later than 11pm, all media off by 10pm, and get up before 7am.

Craig's rule: I will stick to my diet, avoid caffeine after 1pm and alcohol within three hours of bedtime. My rule: I will maintain intermittent fasting protocols (these are explained in the 'Might' section): avoid caffeine after 2pm and alcohol on week nights.

What are your rules? Depending on your personality, think of five to ten codes you can create now to make yourself the man you want to be. Start with your own version of the two above. A code could combine several rules into one. Make it your own, make it meaningful, and think about the benefit you will achieve when you stick to it.

One of the clearest personal rules I had when I was young and heavily into my 'party boy' phase was around alcohol. On many occasions, usually on a lads' holiday, there was a lot of early and all-day drinking going on, so I said, 'I don't drink in the morning.' As I was very clear in my rule, the guys accepted it and we got on with it.

This showed me the power of a rule to improve my life at the time. Without it, I would likely have passed out by the afternoon. Life becomes simpler when you know what you will and won't do as a man.

'As to methods there may be a million and then some, but principles are few. The man who grasps principles can successfully select his own methods. The man who tries methods, ignoring principles, is sure to have trouble.'

RALPH WALDO EMERSON

WHAT ARE YOU WILLING TO SACRIFICE?

TIM MONTGOMERY, USA

Tim Montgomery was the world's fastest man. He made major sacrifices, many mistakes, and ultimately lost sight of his code to achieve his goal.

Tim took Olympic gold in the 2000 Summer Olympics. In 2005, he was found guilty of using performance-enhancing drugs and stripped of his records, including a men's 100 metre world record of 9.78 seconds set in 2002. After retiring from athletics, he was tried and convicted of fraud and dealing heroin.

To begin the interview, I asked Tim if there was anything he would like to add or take away from his introduction.

'Before I learned what my purpose was, I would've said I want to take some things away. I want to keep everything the way it is. I wouldn't be talking to you today if it wasn't for my past; it has made my present. As a child, I raced on the streets. I'm an alley cat racer that happened to spill over into the Olympic Games.'

No matter what has happened before, our mess is our message, and none of us is without flaws. All we can do is strive to be a better man than we were yesterday.

At nineteen years old, Tim broke the world junior 100 metre record. He weighed 128 pounds and ran 9.96 seconds. He decided to cheat at the age of twenty-eight, some nine years later.

Tim explained that in the streets, when they're racing, people want to get jacked up, so they use narcotics. Using the available drugs, they try to get an edge. As a professional, Tim was seeing guys running 9.8 seconds over and over again with no apparent peak in their season. This was when his doubts about other athletes crept in. In an ultimately individual sport, Tim's internal focus shifted to things outside his control.

'I'm thinking, hey, we all got guns. No one is on the line with a knife. We all got guns. Now that's all about who draws the quickest. I know, it doesn't justify it.'

There are men out there who will do anything to get what they think they want or need. I talk about consequences with Tom Cronin, who was in a *Wolf of Wall Street* type environment, later in the book. For every action there is a reaction. Negative or positive, you choose what type of man you will be and what you're willing to sacrifice.

Everyone makes mistakes. Tim chased his dream and made a bad decision, but it made him who he is today as our mistakes shape us. He now exposes this negative side of sport to help others, something he couldn't do with any credibility if he hadn't been through the 'dark side' in his journey.

What has shaped you, so you are perfectly and uniquely capable for your purpose? You've done what you've done, just as Tim did what he did. More importantly, what are you doing right now and what are you going to do? That's all anyone can do: move forward.

Unfortunately, to make the changes we need to make, the pain of discomfort needs to be great, and for many that means hitting rock bottom. In Tim's case, this was the day he got caught. It is easy to assume he is talking about the day he was revealed to be doping in sport, but it was not then. That was minor compared to the day he was about to be kidnapped and killed by drug dealers, but was arrested instead.

'They sit me down and say, "You know we've saved your life… you remember the night you left the club? You looked back and there was a car," and I said, "Yeah, I remember."

"'Well, they followed you home. We stopped the car. They had guns, ropes, masks and everything inside the car for you. That's the day we decided to go ahead and take you off the streets."

'That's when I knew it was for real. It's either death or prison. Prison saved my life.'

Tim's advice to thrive comes down to free time, something he does not take for granted having recently spent three years locked away. There are 86,400 seconds in a day. If Tim gave you $86,400 every day, would you know how to spend it?

'Know how you will spend your time each and every day. If you don't like what you're doing, change it right now.'

TAKE CARE OF YOUR TOMATOES

'Until we can manage time, we can manage nothing else.'

PETER DRUCKER, AUTHOR OF *PEOPLE AND PERFORMANCE*

'Championships are scheduled.' This is a saying of my good friend, ex-baseball professional and the Mental Locker Founder, Tim Dixon. As part of your process to achieve something, you need to schedule in your priorities to get there. It's the same for your ideal life: it's scheduled. It will not just pop up without awareness and strategy. Schedule what you must do daily, weekly and monthly to live it, otherwise you will always be reacting to outside influences.

I schedule important aspects of life on my calendar, including family and social time, which some people think is weird. This time needs to be protected or other stuff will encroach. I break it down to seconds and minutes to build my days.

Schedule your overall winning formula. There are many strategies and tactics you can use, so experiment and nail yours down.

My go-to method to be super productive is the Pomodoro Technique, which got its name from a tomato-shaped timer that its founder, Francesco Cirillo, originally used to sort out his procrastination. I love its simplicity and adaptability to my life to track, produce and focus on the task at hand.

This technique is especially well suited to open and creative type tasks that could go on for ever, leaving you feeling like you have never done enough. I used the technique while writing this book and I am using it right now. Among other things, it helps me take a break mentally at the end of the day with the satisfaction that I have put in the work.

It can feel like you are barely moving, when in reality if you keep turning up with this technique, you will get there. The Pomodoro Technique is basically all about distraction-free single-tasking sprints on steroids (that's just a saying – I am not on steroids).

> '**In a world of distraction,**
> **single-tasking is a superpower.**'
>
> **TIM FERRISS, AUTHOR OF *THE 4-HOUR WORK WEEK***
> **AND *TOOLS OF TITANS***

ACTION 9: POMODORO

Here is the basic 'how to' of the Pomodoro Technique.

Choose a defined task you want to focus on that will take you at least twenty-five minutes to complete. Set your environment to remove as many potential distractions as possible. To start, set your timer for twenty-five minutes (you may end up using thirty to forty minutes in the future), then focus and work like a machine on that one task. That is one Pomodoro.

When the timer finishes, stop (which can be hard sometimes). Have a five-minute break (use the timer), get up, move, get some water/fuel and relax. I sometimes shoot some baskets on the drive (summer) or play some table tennis (winter).

Mark down your Pomodoro on paper with a line, a filled-in box or a tick, and move on to the next Pomodoro. After four Pomodoros, have a longer break of twenty-five minutes, then repeat the process.

For me, marking down the Pomodoros is the crucial part for my feeling of achievement. Track what tasks you are capable of doing in a Pomodoro and how many Pomodoros are realistic in a productive day and week. The most I ever did during the writing of this book was twelve; a productive day was ten. Just remember you can never do half a Pomodoro; you either do one or none.

I have found this consistent practice helps build my discipline. In terms of discipline and process, so many of the high-achieving men I interviewed use some sort of regular meditation. Practices vary from a ten-minute walk, conscious 'four-breath' approach that I favour on route to exercise each morning, to twenty minutes meditation or more twice a day. I also use headphones and different music to get myself in the zone for different tasks. For example, anything by composer Hans Zimmer, especially the *Inception* and *Interstellar* movie soundtracks, was my zone for writing this book. For a shorter project or clients, the *Gladiator*, *The Dark Knight* or *Man of Steel* soundtrack (all also by Hans Zimmer) is my go-to musical accompaniment – did I mention that I love a good movie?

Our own soundtracks are anchored to a specific emotion and meaning for each of us. Be aware and use this to your advantage to get into your best state to perform.

I will talk in more detail about getting into your zone and meditation in Act III – Ascension.

PERSPECTIVE

'Keep constant guard over your perceptions,
for it is no small thing you are protecting, but
your respect, trustworthiness and steadiness,
peace of mind, freedom from pain
and fear, in a word your freedom.
For what would you sell these things?'

EPICTETUS, GREEK STOIC PHILOSOPHER

A PERFECT WORLD

Let's think for a minute. There is nothing wrong with the world, just your view of it. Everything is perfect.

What?

I found this a hard concept to swallow, especially with the wars and carnage going on all over the planet. But if you burden yourself and focus on the negatives of the world, how will that make you feel? Will you be able to live, perform and have a positive impact at a high level? Will you be happy?

My own example is not a life or death scenario, but if I think of my pole-vaulting accident, at the time it definitely was *not* perfect. How could it be? It ruined my knee, my pole-vaulting career, and damaged my physical and mental wellbeing for years to come.

If I look back at my pole-vaulting accident with the perspective of time, I can see how it fits into the story of my life. If I hadn't fully committed on that day, the domino effect would not have got me here. In the story of my life, nothing is perfect, but it is perfectly balanced. Through the adversity, the mental and physical pain, I have been strengthened. I had to adapt, find a new path, a new mission. Life was good before, but now I am able to thrive and appreciate life more after being through the dark days.

We all have problems and adversity to overcome. In this sense, you are not a unique snowflake.

The quality of your life will come back to how you see your problems: the unavoidable challenges to your happiness. I call it the iStruggle scenario. When people are stuck and struggling through life, they see their problems as:

- Indestructible – problems cannot be broken or overcome; they are permanent
- Inescapable – people cannot escape the problem in any way, shape or form
- Individual – their problems are unique to them; no one else has their problem

This helps people justify how others have overcome their problems because they did not have the same 'unique' problem.

> 'There are so many people who have lived and died before you. You will never have a new problem... Somebody wrote the answer down in a book somewhere.'
>
> **WILL SMITH, HOLLYWOOD ACTOR, PRODUCER, AND SONGWRITER**

ACTION 10: EXPECT

What are your current expectations in life? Write and complete the following sentence four times:

One of my expectations in life is...

Drawing one expectation from your list, complete this sentence:

The strongest expectation I have for my life is...

We meet our own expectations. Many times, when others have expectations for us, high or low, we end up meeting them, too. When I think back to my parents' and teachers' expectations, I'm thankful they expected a lot out of me. I always had high expectations for my students as a teacher, and one of the reasons my coaching clients achieve a lot is because I expect them to.

If your expectations are positive and exciting, that's awesome. They must be – they are driving you to a quality future. If any of your expectations are negative, bleak, or just plain ordinary, you need to change. You need to demand more from yourself. I would.

We all have certain specific expectations for our lives. If we are unhappy, it is most likely we are not meeting our own expectations for where we 'should' be at this stage. Sounds simple, but if your expectations are not negative and you are meeting or exceeding them in your current life, you'll be one happy dude.

BRULES TO SUCCESS

What the hell are brules? Simply put, they are 'bullshit rules' that we all enclose ourselves in at some point. In our head, these brules become entrenched. They run in the background of the decisions we make, and we don't take time to question them. If we did sit down to list them out on paper with logical reasons as to why they might not be true, we would realise they are a bullshit perspective.

Success has no set rules. It does not discriminate. People have it with little effort, lots of effort, positive thinking, negative thinking – success can come to us all in many different ways. I am not saying crack on with low effort and negative thinking; I am just making the point that even if you don't have all your ducks in a row, you can still achieve a great deal.

For some, what could be seen as weak or negative, based on traditional 'rules of success', is actually why they end up being so successful. Think of the naturally pessimistic comedian or songwriter who has made it to the top – would they have made it if 'positive thinker' was one of their strengths?

Considering I co-authored *The New Rules of Success* in 2013, I see the irony. The brules we all have to varying extremes can make it seem like we're trying to accelerate towards happiness, but we still have the handbrake on. Before we put pedal to the metal by doing more, we need to release our handbrake.

What brules do you hold yourself back with? Success does leave clues. That is what this book is all about, but ultimately you can do it with what you have, and do it your way. There are always reasons, mostly self-imposed limitations, why people don't change, but when the need becomes a must, you will.

ACTION 11: THE TRIPOD

I love this tripod exercise which I came across through my work with Brian Grasso, the Founder of The Mindset Performance Institute. Brian's podcast was episode number one of *Awaken Your Alpha* back in early 2014, and I have known him now for almost ten years.

This is a simple exercise to throw doubt on your limiting beliefs by providing a counter argument to the 'I will never' statements running through your mind (which will end up being true if you don't tackle them). Basically, we all have our own lens through which we view the world, and this narrow camera frame is filled with our 'I will never' statements.

1. **Limiting reflection.** Complete three 'I will never...' statements.

2. **Absolute truth.** For each, give three reasons why you believe this. These are the three tripod legs holding up your belief.

3. **Counter argument.** Now give three reasons why each belief may not be true. Imagine you are in a court of law, aiming to create reasonable doubt.

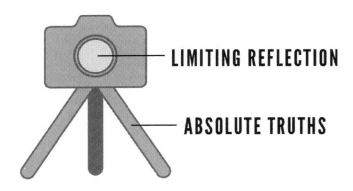

LIMITING REFLECTION

ABSOLUTE TRUTHS

By going through this exercise, you will become aware of where your belief system is held up by stories, experiences and social proof. This can start to release any delusions, planting the seeds of alternatives to your truth and helping to reprogram your unconscious. Convert your 'reality' into just a story by breaking one or more of the tripod legs (the reason/s you believe it to be true). This will move your lens, shifting your view on what is possible and allowing your fixation to go elsewhere.

You may have a problem with this if you have really strong beliefs about a subject, like religion or politics, because you end up not even listening to your counter statements. You already have your 'absolute truth' and you are sticking to it. This fixed mindset will not help you grow as a man. Our stories become our centre and we become them.

'One person's craziness is another person's reality.'

TIM BURTON, OSCAR-WINNING FILM DIRECTOR

OPPORTUNITIES ARE NOT IMMORTAL

LANCE ALLRED, USA

Your opportunities are all around you. The more overworked, stressed and run down you are, the less likely you are to see them.

These opportunities are not immortal. The lifespan of the majority, if not all of them, is unknown. You have to commit not just to pursuing the opportunity, but to getting the most out of each you decide to run with.

> 'Do not go gentle into that good night...rage, rage against the dying of the light.'
>
> **DYLAN THOMAS, POET AND WRITER**

With every basketball team Lance Allred played for, he put this Dylan Thomas quote up in his locker. Lance was born with 80% hearing loss. Throughout his life, people have been placing limitations on him. Eventually, through his own will and choice, he went on to become the first deaf player in NBA history. Known as the Lion, he's also a bestselling Author and TEDx Speaker.

> 'If me, a deaf kid, can put my hearing aids in every day, push myself outside my comfort zone and travel around the world for ten years playing basketball on every continent except Antarctica, what is anyone else's excuse not to push themselves beyond their comfort zone and do something new? Everyone thinks they want the American dream, but what price are they willing to pay for it?'

To achieve anything great, you have to be willing to be uncomfortable, and Lance developed a high threshold for discomfort. Growing up in a polygamist community, Lance lived in a monogamous home with one mum, but it was normal for his friends to have three or four mums. His father was expected to be a patriarch of a polygamous group, the Allred group, but he came upon the knowledge that several of the leaders had been sexually abusing kids for years. Lance's parents were the only ones who left.

> 'I had to work so hard to be able to speak. Communication is the thing I am most grateful for, but it's also the thing that most people take for granted. My parents showed me a lot of how to awaken your alpha and never be afraid to speak the truth.'

Lance's former community was angry, and his family went into hiding. That year, in eighth grade at a new school, he grew from 5 foot 10 inches to 6 foot 4. The school basketball coach asked him to play for the team, bearing in mind that Lance had never played basketball before.

> 'I just wasn't considered an athletic kid; all I did was play Nintendo, Dungeons and Dragons – cool stuff like that.'

He had to keep his hearing aids out due to sweating and concussion issues, and in his very first game, he was ejected. The referee thought Lance was ignoring him.

It didn't deter him.

> 'I was a big man. Also, with my back to the basket, I could see all the other nine players and I had to do the talking. I wasn't the greatest jumper, so I ran really fast. It's choice if you just want to run your guts out every time.'

During our interview, Lance's perseverance and grit came across. He had been carrying around his own brules from his childhood. At the age of five, he had been told by a Sunday School teacher that

God had made him deaf as a form of punishment; that he had done something wrong in the pre-existence. Lance still had this story in his head as a man.

We all have so much baggage from other people and our environment that we take it into our adult lives. We're largely operating from that foundation, so we need to be open to the fact that the foundation is likely flawed. Lance told himself the story that he had to be the first deaf player in NBA history and then God would love him.

The average NBA player is drafted when they're twenty or twenty-one. Lance was twenty-four when he finished college, so people were already saying he was too old. That senior year, he led the nation in rebounding, but got only one NBA workout, so for his first contract, he went to Istanbul. He then went on to a Spanish team, but injured his knee and the team wouldn't pay for his treatment.

He went home in debt, sleeping on his parents' sofa and paying for his own rehab. The next year, he got one job offer to play up in Boise, Idaho in the NBA Development League, making $900 a month. At that point, many a man would have turned it down to get a 'real job'.

> 'I stuck it out and I didn't play for about six weeks because I was just a token guy at the end of the bench who did all the media stuff. They thought I wasn't good enough to play. I'm turning twenty-six in weeks. I am stressed out.'

Within one week, the starting centre broke his leg, the reserve starting centre got recalled to the Seattle Supersonics, and, by default, Lance became the starting centre. The coach was stressed out and told Lance, 'We just signed somebody today who will be here tomorrow, but tonight you've got to start. I know you haven't played in a while, so play safe, keep it simple, get some rebounds, maybe get two or four points.'

Lance had his opportunity. He had known that if he kept putting in and putting in, he would get one shot. He made sure that when it came, he was ready to take it.

'My practice time was my game time for that season. Even if my teammates didn't need me on the fast break, I was going to sprint with them. I would go further and touch the baseline every time. My teammates laughed at me; they thought I was being ridiculous. But when my number was called that game, my first game as a starter, I gave them thirty points and ten rebounds, and I was able to play forty-eight minutes because I believe for every action [there] is an equal and opposite reaction.'

From there, Lance set the D League on fire, averaging twenty-two points and thirteen rebounds a game. His coach got a call, and Lance was called up to play with the Cleveland Cavaliers and LeBron James. Lance not only made history as the first deaf player in the NBA, but just as inspiring to me, he did not make it until he was twenty-seven.

His vision was clear. As Lance explained, every goal he has ever written down has come true.

'Every goal I write down I put above my light switch, and every time I touch my light switch I have to read it three times. 95% of the world will stop reading their goals because their intuition could tell them what they need to do, but that's too much hard work. I've never felt entitled to anything. I never felt I was owed anything.'

That first season Lance got to the NBA playoffs, but then in 2008, the economy collapsed. Most teams were releasing players to save money, and Lance was no exception.

> 'You have a dream, it's amazing, but then also it's like, "Wait, why don't I feel any different? I'm here, I've achieved my dream. Why don't I feel like somehow God loves me more?" I had been doing this whole foolish game of attaching my self-worth to an outcome. Whether it's a new job, a new car, or a new lover, that will complete me, and that's a lie; that's an illusion. These are hard lessons, hard experiences, extremely high heights with extremely low lows that have really brought me to this quintessential truth. Love is either unconditional or it is not love at all, and my self-worth is never attached to any outcome.'

As Lance did, you too will get your shot. At that time, it is too late to get ready; you must *be* ready. You cannot turn apparent weaknesses into strengths, liabilities into assets, unless you are willing and able to endure the darker times. Endurance and relentlessness are key to seeing the light on the other side.

Many men know how to thrive in the great times. It is the other times, the tough times that separate true grit from the appearance of grit. You do not have to conquer others; you only need to be tough with yourself. Conquer yourself and the rest will align.

'Nothing in the world can take the place of persistence. Talent will not; nothing is more common than unsuccessful men with talent. Genius will not; unrewarded genius is almost a proverb. Education will not; the world is full of educated derelicts. Persistence and determination alone are omnipotent.'

CALVIN COOLIDGE, THIRTIETH PRESIDENT OF THE UNITED STATES

THE #1 DESTRUCTIVE EMOTION

'Fear is to a man's soul as a drop of
poison is to a well of spring water.'

CHIN-NING CHU, AUTHOR OF *THICK FACE, BLACK HEART*

When I find myself lying awake at night, it's usually not because my neighbours are up to a bit of overly enthusiastic 'horizontal jogging' (although that has happened). It's the fear of not being enough for my wife, my family, my challenges, my mission, and even this book; the ambition of wanting to do and be more for myself and others.

The fear of not being enough will affect your behaviours on a deep level, and can become a constant force of resistance. I know I've spent too long there. When this fear pops into your head, it's time to stop pussyfooting around. It's time to grab life by the balls and awaken your alpha, my friend.

Let's get things into perspective. 'What's the most dangerous job you have?' That was the question James Butler (man on a mission) walked into an Armed Forces recruiting office with, straight from school. At that stage, he didn't know what he wanted, but he was clear about what he didn't want: he was afraid of being mediocre: 'It was like my fear of being mediocre far surpassed my fear of dying.'

The fear of being normal, forgotten, and having a life of no significance is one I share, and you may, too. For James, he ended up with explosives strapped to him, swimming underwater at night, diffusing bombs and blowing up bridges.

Fear can be the most destructive emotion in a man. Most of the time, the majority of us don't even know what we are afraid of, but generally, it boils down to either a fear of success or a fear of failure. The crazy thing is, our fear of success is greater than our fear of failure, which is why many of us fail to achieve the life we're capable of.

In life, it is usually not acceptable to admit our biggest fear. It is more common to answer this question without deep thought and pass it off with a bland answer, a bit like when someone asks us if we're OK. Most of us say yes, regardless of whether we're doing great or depressed.

What are you really afraid of? Could you easily write it down? If you could, great, but it is more likely you need to spend time identifying exactly what it is you're afraid of, and why. Is it public speaking? Calling someone? Putting yourself out there? Launching that business? By really being able to define your fear, you go a long way towards being able to conquer it.

We are born with only two fears: the fear of falling and the fear of loud noises. We pick up the rest along the way. Fear holds most of us back from fully doing our thing, and (at least for me) it can cause a constant internal battle.

The Stoic Philosophers of ancient Greece approached fear by exploring worst-case scenarios, or '*the premeditation of evils*' as they phrased it. If you believe you are truly fearless at this point, crack straight on to Part II. For the rest of us, what follows is a valuable process.

ACTION 12: PREMEDITATION OF EVILS

This is initially about using negative visualisation to position where you are now in a positive perspective. The questions of 'What would it actually be like if it all hit the fan?' and 'What would that feel like?' increase your awareness and gratitude for now. The more realistic consequences of a decision are illuminated by exploring the worst ones.

This is not to be confused with always focusing on worst-case scenarios without realistic assessment or thought. It is *vital* to clarify the difference.

Overly focusing on what you don't want to happen as a lifestyle is a mistake. Premeditating worst case outcomes inside a process helps keep negative thoughts in perspective, and is a useful tool. It enables you to make bold decisions and move forward in whatever direction you chose.

Draw your own premeditation of evils quadrant using two lines across a blank page, splitting it into four sections. For a specific 'big thing' you are thinking about doing or have been unsure about for some time, answer these key questions in the four spaces.

Extreme negatives. What's the very worst that could happen if you did it? What doubts and feelings come to mind? How permanent would this outcome be? Attach a percentage to how likely these things are to happen.

Recovery. How could you get things back under control if you had to? To repair the damage, what would you need to do to get back to or close to normality?

Potential positives. What are the likely positive outcomes, both internal and external? Again, using a percentage rating, what would be the impact of these outcomes? What do you believe is the chance of even a slightly good outcome? Note this as a percentage.

Do nothing. What price will you pay internally and externally for not taking action? Calculate your cost of inaction. Not doing things because of fear of failure is an issue that will magnify over the years. Where will this decision (or lack thereof) project you in eighteen months and eighteen years from now? Just as doing something has a consequence, doing nothing often has far greater consequences.

This process is a powerful, measured and logical approach that brings to light the cost of inaction. Doing nothing is the riskiest course of action, worst-case scenarios are unlikely, and the majority can be repaired with bold action (the default setting of high-achieving men). If you retreat to 'waiting for the right time' instead of a yes or a no, that is an excuse we all have used, and it is bollocks. It just means you're not a robot and you're afraid, like the rest of us.

It sounds clichéd, but it works to do something each day that is outside your comfort zone. Some of the biggest breakthroughs come when your back is against the wall and the only way out is to go forward through the fear. So, figure out your fears and keep developing your courage to act in spite of them.

'We suffer more often in imagination than in reality.'

SENECA, ROMAN STOIC PHILOSOPHER

SUMMARY

'Life is not primarily a quest for pleasure, as Freud believed, or a quest for power as Alfred Adler taught, but a quest for meaning. The greatest task for any person is to find meaning in his or her life.'

VIKTOR E FRANKL, AUTHOR OF *MAN'S SEARCH FOR MEANING*

- Do the work to gain clarity on who you are and why you are where you are now
- Who is the man you want to become and what must you do to become that man?
- What are your priorities now and in the long term?
- What are the agreements and codes you live by?
- Commit to clarifying your mission (if you have not yet done so) and decide on specific tactics you are going to implement to get you heading in the right direction. You cannot stay still

ACT II

ACTION

'All courses of action are risky, so prudence is not in avoiding danger (it's impossible), but calculating risk and acting decisively. Make mistakes of ambition and not mistakes of sloth. Develop the strength to do bold things, not the strength to suffer.'

NICCOLÒ MACHIAVELLI, ITALIAN PHILOSOPHER

I will be breaking 'Action' down into:

MIND
MOMENTUM
MIGHT
MOOLA

In this section you will:

- Identify actionable tactics to execute

- Do something with your bucket list rather than waiting until you think you're closer to the end of your life

- Become clear what your limiting beliefs are costing you and your loved ones

- Begin the process of replacing these beliefs with ones that empower you

- Identify where you need to adopt a hunter's mentality towards your current opportunities – what do you need to do to optimise and manage your energy?

- Develop your money mindset, habits and actions to move towards your financial freedom

MIND

'If we did all the things we are capable of doing,
we would literally astound ourselves.'

THOMAS EDISON

THE MOVING DEADLINE

I believe strongly in the power of deadlines. You may know you
are not the person who can do the 'thing' today, but having given
yourself a deadline, you are now committed to change and evolve.

Do the steps to become the man you need to be as quickly as
possible. With awareness of who you are, what you want and why
you are not quite there yet, you are ready to clarify exactly what
you are shooting for. Write it down and say it aloud. You *must*
commit to it. Tell friends and family.

With this commitment, which is the action of making your 'thing'
real, impose immovable deadlines on yourself. You could pay
money to enter a race in three months' time that you know you
couldn't do today. You could secure a TEDx talk and then work
out what you are actually going to say – that one sticks in the
mind for me. It may be a small thing, it may be something large,
but get in the habit of setting deadlines.

On 8 October 2010, my first son Dylan was born. My wife and
I had held a vision to move to the United States at some time for

some time, but now we committed to a deadline to move before Dylan started school. We didn't know any details, which was a good thing, but we did know we had five years to make it happen.

It was a huge mission, involving mountains of paperwork, financial commitments, reorganising our careers – ultimately, going all in. Roughly five years later, on 1 September 2015, I captured a photo of both my boys (our second son Harrison was two years old) looking out of the window towards the plane at Heathrow Airport in London. This is such a powerful photo for me as I had visualised the scene and been convinced it was inevitable.

We landed in the United States and Dylan started school the next week.

With this sort of inevitability thinking and a why that is strong enough, you will make a way to meet your deadline. If your why is not strong enough, you won't. (I will dig more into the process and strategy in the coming chapters.) If you always wait until you're 'fully ready', you're already late, or that time may never happen.

If you commit to deadlines, but let them pass, what other opportunities will pass you by? Will your vision consistently be on the back burner? Will you be dead before you reach your deadline?

EXECUTE THE BUCKET

'When I say tomorrow, I now experience myself as someone who puts things off and the integrity of me as a powerful man is gone. Chances are many people will die tomorrow, many people will die today, but the worst part is that many of us will live for a very long time in a disempowered state.'

JAMES G. BUTLER (1989–2017)

When we make a bucket list, we tend to lean towards the comforting assumption that we have plenty of time before we die, wrinkly and fulfilled, at some point far off in the future. The reality is no one knows when they'll die, so that mindset is too risky, too long term, and usually means that our bucket list doesn't get done.

Age is a loose guide as to when our time will be up. Too many of my close friends and family, old and young, have gone, taking too many great ideas and unexperienced adventures with them. Kick the bucket list out; get rid of it. Tomorrow is not a given; when you say tomorrow, you experience yourself as weak – 'I said no to my big thing, so who am I for my wife, for my partner? Who am I for my children? Who am I for my work?' The ripple effect shows up everywhere in your life.

Nothing triggers me to react like hearing a man blame his wife and kids for holding him back. If you put the ownership on to your partner, you'll end up resenting them with no idea why. I will not waste space here with a long list of legendary men who have achieved great things while having a fulfilled family life. You must be strong enough to enrol your partner in something you believe in.

BACK YOURSELF

JOHN BLAKE, AUSTRALIA

'Back yourself' are the words John lives by, and when you hear his story, they will become all the more powerful.

I first connected with John through a mastermind group. Then by coincidence we were both in Las Vegas at the same time and had the chance to meet up. John was actually in the third episode I used to launch the podcast back in 2014, and some 300+ episodes later, I did not hesitate to include his story in this book.

For the last twenty-five years, John has been in sales. His experience – having to overcome adversity, fight daily resistance and back himself – continues to be inspirational to me. Eight years ago, he set up a consulting business with a partner, helping salespeople to fast-track their knowledge and results.

He describes how they were being booked in the early years.

'Day three of a conference, a room full of salespeople with a screaming hangover, after a massive barbecue lunch, their blood sugar levels in their underpants, and you're somehow expected, after a one-hour presentation, to turn them into masterful salespeople.'

John remembers sitting in the terminal of Sydney Airport. He had dealt with about seventy-five clients during that past year, so he decided to rank them and select the bottom half. This amounted to almost forty clients that he then deleted to see what it would do to the business's bottom line.

'Eleven per cent. I sort of looked at it and went, "Holy crap!" We could have dealt with half the clients, done half the work, and really, we would have ended up doing more business. We would have been able to focus and look after that top 50% better.'

John made this a reality within days. The average transaction size of the business went from AU$7,000 a client up to about AU$50,000 within sixty to ninety days. Obviously, this took a massive shift in mindset, but the financial aspect swiftly followed.

ACTION 14: A BETTER WAY?

Essentially, there were a few key things John did. Firstly, as soon as he realised there was a better way of doing business, he stepped boldly into action and backed himself to transform everything. He created two or three high-value packages to get results, then modified his sales process so his ongoing support package was a no brainer for clients. From a business standpoint, he was now able to attract like-minded clients by only focusing on his ideal client.

Is there a better way to do what you are currently doing? How could you package things differently? What could you change to get the best results for all involved?

As great as this was for John, it wasn't this that awakened his alpha. It was more a set of circumstances that were thrown at him, forcing him to step up and deal with them in the most powerful way he knew.

'It was a culmination of a whole bunch of things that happened all at once. My wife actually passed away three years ago. To add to that, at the time she left me with a five-month-old son and a three-year-old daughter. I also moved house and launched a new business all within a fourteen-week period.'

When bad things happen, it's what we do next, how we fight for our lives, that defines us. Unless you have gone through that before, you won't know exactly how you will feel and deal with it.

'I felt like every day I was pulling on the armour, grabbing the sword, going out and battling... all the stuff that was just going on. So that's essentially what forced me to become strong. It was that period of my life. You know… if I can pop out the other end of that, I mean, there are not too many things that are going to rattle me.'

The more you back yourself, the bolder you are, the more you will be prepared to back yourself. At the end of the day, the only person you can really rely upon to back you is you.

ACTION 15: THE DICKENS PROCESS

In one of the first men's workshops I did in England, I included this exercise to deal with the question: what are your beliefs costing you? The Dickens process is a neuro-linguistic programming (NLP) technique based on *A Christmas Carol* by Charles Dickens. I first came across it thanks to Tim Ferriss, who had spoken about going through it at a Tony Robbins event.

This is a powerful process and a great one to repeat annually. I will give you the essentials to complete.

Examine your top two to three current limiting beliefs using the format explained below. In *A Christmas Carol*, Scrooge is visited by ghosts of the past, present and future, hence the name of the process. For each belief, answer the following, remembering it is important to see, feel, hear and describe your responses in detail, as you get out what you put in:

Past. What has the belief cost you? How has it affected the people you were close to? What have you missed out on/ lost?

Present. What is your belief costing you and the people close to you now?

Future. What will it have cost you and the people you're close to in one, three, five and ten years' time?

By being honest and really feeling the pain that has come from the beliefs in this exercise, you can't avoid or skip any timescale and impact on your life. Usually it's too easy to revert to 'It'll get better' or 'This is how it is' without identifying what's holding you back and what it really means to you.

OVERCOMING DEPRESSION

'The happiness of your life depends
upon the quality of your thoughts.'

MARCUS AURELIUS, ROMAN EMPEROR

This is a chapter I could have quite easily missed out, and that is part of the problem. We avoid talking about depression, my former self included (but clearly I have got better at it). In society, if you break a bone, or ruin your knee as I did, everyone rallies around to ask you about it. The injury is clear to see, easy to explain, easy to understand, and the recovery process can be quite straightforward. But tell people you're depressed and you are likely to get the complete opposite reaction. People will back away.

Why do we accept that other body parts break down at times, but not our brains? This has created a culture that doesn't understand mental health. Men especially sweep depression under the carpet because 'real' men have a strong mindset and depression is for the weak, right?

Wrong.

Depression hit me pretty hard a year after my pole-vaulting accident. Having gone down that road, I respect depression too much to underplay it and believe I am immune to it now, and one of the key reasons why I am roughly seven years clear of depression is awareness. By acknowledging it's there, I have learned from the past which circumstances, habits and early warning signs will come back given half a chance. However, I have intentionally included depression in the 'Action' section instead of the 'Awareness' section because it is the actions, routines, processes and tactics spread throughout this book that will weaken it.

When you are really depressed, it is a tough place to be. For me, it was a long slope that I gradually slipped down over the course of a year before I finally hit rock bottom. I was stuck there for around a year, and during that time I wanted so badly to be happy, but I could not get out of my own head. I couldn't even 'escape' to enjoy a film, and I have always been a big movie lover.

Dealing with excessive stress is something I talk more about in Part III with Tom Cronin. The key thing to grasp is that everyone has the ability to make their way back to happiness. As Tom puts it:

'I was a drug addict, I was suffering clinical depression, I was suicidal. It doesn't matter how far gone you are, everyone has the ability to rewrite their part, to get back on orbit. The further off orbit [you are], obviously the longer it is going take to get back into orbit. You can get back in orbit real quick, it just takes a shift in lifestyle, a shift in the model.'

If you do the things I've highlighted and talked about in this book when you are feeling like crap and really don't want to, it will go a long way to preventing you from slipping all the way down the slope into deep depression. I am sure you can think of a set of circumstances that even the most mentally tough person would struggle in. Sure, everyone has varied levels of susceptibility to depression. If you have ever heard of Seasonal Affective Disorder – or SAD – that is how it emerged early on for me. Even if I was not depressed, I did get pretty low in the darker months each year, so I pre-empted it by scheduling certain activities or events during this time. January or February are great times to attend events that will better you, especially in somewhere sunny like California.

In late 2009, after a year of traumatic events back to back and a healthy dose of denial, I was in a bad place. I was shutting down and becoming isolated. My rock-bottom moment was when my mum turned up on my doorstep and I lost it; I didn't have the energy to cover it up any more.

I still felt like an absolute loser for a long time to come, but gradually from this point I was getting better. It doesn't matter if it is a huge leap or a millimetre, better is better. This is the same whether you're struggling or you're thriving, and why, and that is why I truly believe in life, you are either growing or dying. You cannot stand still; trying to maintain the status quo is a mistake. For everyone, the path out of the hole, the path to recovery, is different. There is no one set answer.

'The divine guidance often comes when
the horizon is the blackest.'

MAHATMA GANDHI

Like the seasons, one thing in life is certain, its ever-changing nature. Animals appear to understand and deal with this better than the majority of humans. One of my favourite aspects of moving to the wilderness of Northern Michigan is the connection I have with clear seasons, embracing each one for what it brings.

Friends ask, 'Oh, what about the winters there?' to which I respond, 'It's better than rain. I can do something with snow – I love it!' Would you really appreciate an eternal summer, with blistering temperatures and no variation in weather every day? Would I appreciate snow being here for twelve months? Hell, no. I love the fun activities, skiing, the landscape, and the play that comes with having kids + snow combined. Then when April comes around, I am more than ready to see the grass again. By the end of summer, I am excited to see the stunning 'Michigan Colours' of the autumn (fall) before heading into winter again.

In life, change is coming. You can either panic, complain about it, or embrace the changes, challenges and opportunities each season brings. Always focusing on what you can't do is a sure-fire way to miss out on what you can do.

> 'If you are distressed by anything external, the pain is not due to the thing itself, but to your estimate of it; and this you have the power to revoke at any moment.'
>
> **MARCUS AURELIUS, ROMAN EMPEROR**

ACTION 16: A POSITIVE ALTERNATIVE

You identified the impact of your limiting beliefs in the last exercise (the Dickens process), and learned how to remove and discredit these beliefs in the tripod exercise. Now let's start to replace them with something that will do you a favour in life.

Rewrite the positive alternative for two to three of your existing limiting beliefs. For example, one of my top limiting beliefs was 'More money means you are greedy' and I replaced that with 'More money means you are helping more people'. This may sound or feel silly, but go through the process anyway. Replace each limiting belief, write the new belief in a place where you will see and read it aloud every morning for a month, then see how you feel.

MOMENTUM

'Sometimes thinking too much can
destroy your momentum.'

**TOM WATSON, PROFESSIONAL GOLFER AND
OLDEST MAN TO BREAK PAR IN THE MASTERS**

AMERICAN MUSCLE CARS

Think of the great old American 'muscle cars': big, beautiful, powerful things, but with little or no power steering. If you turn the steering wheel to change course when the car is stationary, you'd better be built like Arnold Schwarzenegger as it's near impossible. But if you take a little action, put your foot on to the pedal and start moving in the right direction, then once you're up to speed, the steering wheel becomes lighter and you can adjust as you go.

Once you have momentum, don't underestimate it; gather and use it. When you're moving forward with momentum, the landscape will change quickly, new opportunities will arise, so stay open, but keep your vision in mind. Failures, or 'learning experiences' as I prefer to call them, will happen faster too, so don't dwell on them or let them slow you down.

One common trait I have observed in the many successful men I've interviewed is their attitude to failure. It is very different to that of the average man. The masses will stop after one, two, maybe three failures when they're trying to accomplish anything, but the success could have been waiting for the fourth attempt. The successful are relentless in their pursuit of their objective, and many times their achievement comes long after most people would have deemed it reasonable to quit.

To put it simply, lack of momentum equals lack of results in life.

'No human ever became interesting by not failing; the more you fail and recover and improve, the better you are as a person. Ever meet someone who's always had everything work out for them with zero struggle? They usually have the depth of a puddle or they don't exist.'

CHRIS HARDWICK, STAND-UP COMEDIAN AND TV HOST

Don't be blind to opportunities and always say yes to the ambitious life you're striving to create. But be clear and realistic about what you want your life to be and what you're willing to do to achieve it. It is also powerful to say no to anything that does not align with the direction of your vision. Don't just follow someone else's definition of a successful life. Sure, David Beckham and Richard Branson have achieved a lot, but their lives are likely different from yours or mine.

Many publicly successful men have countless restrictions and demands on their time. To create a persona that they now feel they have to maintain, did they sacrifice too much? Is the 'freedom' you're after really freedom?

Start saying yes to people, places and ideas that move you towards your vision. Don't just live a cautious life where you arrive at the end unscathed.

BECOMING THE HUNTER

'If it bleeds, we can kill it.'

ARNOLD SCHWARZENEGGER, PREDATOR 1987

Are you waiting for your next meal or are you going out to catch it? Quite simply, this is the hunter versus lurker mentality. OK, I admit I'll do anything to get another line from Arnold in there, and *Predator* is my favourite film of all time. However, there is a point to it.

In this classic movie, there comes a critical time where the group are getting picked off one by one en route to the helicopter rescue. It is clear no one will survive if they continue this way, so they decide to stop, take back control of their own lives and become the hunter.

Do you let life pick away at you until there is nothing left? Do you lurk around waiting for opportunities to come to you? Make a stand now, before it's too late. Get out of your own way and hunt down and create opportunities to thrive.

A great example of this in action is action movie star Silvio Simac (see what I did there?) who I cover in more depth later in this chapter. In his first film, he was actually hired as a stuntman and spent the first three weeks on set in Thailand doing absolutely nothing. The stunt coordinator was Yuen Woo-ping, the famous director who choreographed the *Matrix* trilogy (Silvio has worked with him on four features since).

Three weeks in, bored and disappointed, Silvio pulled the director to the side and said, 'Why can't I be in the movie?' He showed him some of his moves; the director actually wrote his role into the film there and then.

You need to be the hunter.

Sure, Silvio had dry seasons, as you will too. Life for all of us is uncertain, despite the illusion of stability we try to create for ourselves. Silvio gave up his safe former career, as I did, to force himself to succeed in a new arena. The alpha is a hunter and doesn't become complacent.

The longer you persist on your mission, the more you're differentiating yourself from the herd. How many people are relentless and mentally strong when things get tough? It's a small list. What I like most about Silvio's example is that he was not satisfied just to be a passenger on his first movie. He didn't settle for that; he created his opportunity to run.

Many times, it is easier to put something off than to make a decision over it. But if you don't make a decision, you actually mean 'no' without having the balls to say it. An opportunity will not hang around for ever, but too many of us get stuck into thinking that we can always make the decision 'Tomorrow' or 'When I am ready'.

Make decisions quickly and be slow to change your mind when others doubt your big plans (which they will). You know what you're capable of. Strive for progress, not perfection. It must be a 'Hell, yes' or a 'Hell, no'; it is the maybes in life that kill us all.

ACTION 17: HUNT OR HOLD

First, identify all the areas – situations, people, opportunities – you are currently waiting on. This is your 'hold on' list. Then, assess how these areas have affected your growth. What do you feel you have missed out on? You may previously have been a hunter to get an opportunity, but now find yourself lingering and not making the most of it.

Finally, if you decided to go on the 'hunt' in all the areas you have identified, what effect would that have? What are the one to three specific actions you can do for each to become the hunter?

Don't just wait for the opportunities to come to you then ambush them. Get out there on the hunt. Make a simple plan and do one action to start this today.

EARN THE RIGHT TO TRUST YOUR GUT

CHARLIE 'THE SPANIARD' BRENNEMAN, USA

As with life, competing in the sports arena is very different to being on the sidelines watching someone else compete. This leads me to former UFC (Ultimate Fighting Championship) fighter Charlie 'The Spaniard' Brenneman. His story of what you can accomplish by making the most of your opportunities is legendary.

Before Charlie decided to pursue the UFC, he was a junior high Spanish teacher. He had wrestled his whole life, but then he (in his own words) 'got into a comfortable position. Nice job, nice salary, nice comfortable spot in my hometown'. Then he had his awakening and thought, 'I really want to do that. I want to pursue the UFC', so he did. He left the security of his job and chased his dream, making a plan, putting in the work and eventually getting to where he wanted to go.

I asked Charlie what moment he knew he had to go all in for his dream.

'It was a very definitive moment. I saw a friend of mine… Frankie as a top mixed martial artist and it was like a light bulb went off in my head. I thought, wait a minute, I wrestled with him, I touched him. If he can do it, I can too.'

Charlie makes a great point here. Too many people put others on pedestals, like they are from a different world or something. The reality is, if you're not going to do something, someone else is going to do it. If you want it, get involved and be that man.

As with all the guests in this book, Charlie had a clear mission. Getting to the UFC was his vision and goal, so he started fighting, and everything he did from that point forward led him there.

'My first fight was in a small town, a cage in the middle of a bunch of drunk people, and I was teaching junior high Spanish at that time. I lost my way a little bit, but I'm a wrestler who learned how to fight. During my early fights when they started to punch me, I was like, "Oh yeah, it's a fight, not a wrestling match".'

> ## 'Everyone has a plan until they get punched in the mouth.'
>
> **MIKE TYSON, YOUNGEST-EVER WORLD HEAVYWEIGHT BOXING CHAMPION**

I love this quote from Mike Tyson. The best time to work life out is when you're in the arena. You learn quickly. Charlie did that and fulfilled his mission to be signed by the UFC.

What makes his story even better is what happened when he got the opportunity. He was scheduled to fight on the undercard, but a main-event fighter was removed for high-level testosterone. 'They needed a sacrificial lamb,' as Charlie put it, and at the last minute, he was asked to step up. Charlie was not even ranked; his opponent, Rick Story, was ranked number six in the world.

Charlie ended up causing one of the biggest upsets in UFC history.

> 'His [Charlie's] fight tonight was a Rocky story.
> He's in his hometown, and he gets the shot at
> the guy who's hot and on his way to a
> title shot. He comes in and wins it.'
>
> **DANA WHITE, PRESIDENT OF THE UFC**

If you do the work needed so you know you're more than capable, when it's time to perform, like Charlie, you'll be able to rely on your gut instinct, and that's going to take you all the way. It is an overused phrase to say, 'Trust your gut', and I don't fully agree with it unless you have worked hard at your craft to understand it first. That's why including the words 'earn the right' is a key distinction.

NOWHERE TO HIDE

These are the highs from the arena Charlie chose, but I found it just as inspiring talking to him about his lows. As men, we get a lot out of dealing with the challenging times that we all face throughout life. When Charlie had a 'bad day at the office', everyone knew about it. A couple of years after his big upset against Rick Story, he got his arse kicked live on television with an overhand one-punch knockout. He was out cold, and sports channels would repeat it in slow motion for years to come.

> 'Stuff is going to happen to you. It was absolutely horrible for me, [but] you can't run, and you can't deny. Two minutes later, I had to stand up next to the guy while they raised his hand. You have to accept that.'

So many times, we shy away, we play small and we hide. Our failures may not be televised, but what bigger arena do we need than to fight for our own lives? We must remind ourselves that shit is going to happen whether we play big or small.

By continually committing to *Awaken Your Alpha*, you will get knocked on your arse far more often than if you play it safe, fact. You will also experience more and achieve more in your life than the average man. If that's the path you are choosing (having this book in your hands is a good sign), you have got to accept these facts and get aligned with the reality. Decide if you are willing to sacrifice your apparent comfort.

The UFC has a rule that if you lose three times, you are out, making it a very high-performing environment. Sure enough, this happened to Charlie, but unlike many others, he managed to come back when most people had written him off.

'I went back to fighting in small places where they were like, "Hey, you're The Spaniard, you're in the UFC, now you're fighting here? What's wrong with you, man?"'

Charlie understood the power of the fundamentals that got him to success the first time. So often, as men we think we have to do exceptional things every day or we have failed. It is the fundamentals, the little things we do daily, that will make us exceptional. Make sure you come back, even if you have literally been knocked down and out.

MIGHT

'It is one thing to study war
and another to live the warrior's life.'

TELAMON OF ARCADIA, MERCENARY OF THE FIFTH CENTURY BC

PROTECT YOUR ENERGY

Everything is energy. You are energy. *The whole point of life is energy.* You bring it to everything you do. How you manage, transfer and use your energy is going to make a difference to everything in this book and your life. Energy is important? No shit, Sherlock!

Sporting a six-pack, looking buff and having great skin are all by-products of creating a body that has an energy output efficient enough to handle all the challenges you will achieve if you decide to do so. As a high-level pole-vaulter, I never worried about all these 'bonuses', as I saw them. I was focused on managing my energy to be able to handle the demands of the training to increase my power output and achieve more.

After pole vaulting, my attitude changed very little in this respect. I approach key events in my life – my TEDx talk, this book – like I used to approach a big competition. I set a deadline, manage my energy, fuel correctly, build, and put in the work daily to be in the best shape to perform. I am just an 'entrepreneurial athlete' now.

Energy is also vital to your charisma and your presence (which I'll speak about more with NLP master David Shepard). Basically, energy follows attention. Wherever your focus goes, your energy flows. This is why it is so important to be present in the moment with others.

To have this positive presence as your 'norm', you need to have plenty of energy. If your body is not prepared for your ambitions, you'll swiftly get knocked on your arse until you take responsibility for developing it.

> 'Do you choose to get back up every time you get knocked down? Simple as that. It's a choice.
> I choose to get back up every time. I know there is no magic wand, there's no cheat sheet to instant fame or success. I want everyone to promise that you [will] choose to get back up every time you get knocked down, one more time, every time.'

LANCE ALLRED, THE FIRST DEAF PLAYER IN NBA HISTORY

BODY FOR ACTION

SILVIO SIMAC, CROATIA AND THE UK

When I think of a man who is ready for action, one name keeps popping up. Silvio Simac started off his journey as a top-class martial artist. He's been World Champion in taekwondo, British Champion fourteen times and European Champion four times. Currently he has black belts in five different systems.

His excellence in martial arts spurred him into movies, working with top people in the business such as Keanu Reeves, Jason

Statham and Jet Li. He's an actor and a man of action – think Jean-Claude Van Damme in the movie *Blood Sport*.

Martial arts is a discipline involving consistency and control of your body and mind. This control came across when I was talking to Silvio.

'In life, one of the things I've come to realise over the years is everything is made up of energy. The more you give, the more you get back. The same with success and the same with prosperity. In any kind of success, any kind of rewards that you get from your work, from your workouts, from whatever, you must first give up a lot of yourself. Give energy first in order to get it back.'

After years of mastering his craft, Silvio was offered his first role in a Hong Kong production filmed in Thailand. As his awakening moment, he realised that the calibre, level and league of this new environment was quite a bit higher than he was used to. He had to package himself differently to succeed.

That's where Silvio's physical development excelled to a different level. His body, his physique and his training changed drastically in order for him to thrive. I asked about his key habits (in addition to physical training), and what came across was his discipline as a lifestyle: staying away from certain foods completely; listening to meditational frequencies and stimulating his subconscious mind for two hours before falling asleep every night, which leads to a positive, fresh state of mind when he wakes up.

I get a similar effect from writing a brief gratitude post in my journal and reading a few pages (of the right stuff) just before bed. You can experiment to find what works for you, but I do believe it is essential to have a routine to achieve this reset.

Silvio's final piece of advice struck a chord with me.

> 'Over the years, some of the stuff I settled for previously, that I thought was good enough, wasn't. People should keep pushing their boundaries. Get out of your comfort zone, expand and grow. What you might think is good by your current standards may not be good by standards further out there. So keep pushing, pursuing, get as much as you can from yourself. Not to the point where your health is suffering, but get out there and give it your all.

> 'Sometimes we get out of our comfort zone, and too quickly we think, I've done enough. I look back at some of my events in life where I thought I did my best at the time, but I really didn't. I could have done a lot more.'

WORLD CHAMPION FUEL

MATT LOVELL, UK

You can't get much more alpha than a World Champion team of rugby-playing warriors. Matt Lovell was the man responsible for the nutrition of the England rugby team that won the 2003 World Cup in Australia. I can still clearly remember the moment – with the time difference, it was weird being let into a pub in the UK at 7am to watch the game.

Matt basically fuels the elite to get the best performances out of their bodies. I wanted to get a slice of that knowledge for the guy who's looking to get the best out of whatever he chooses to do in life.

After university, when Matt realised what he actually wanted to do, he retrained as a Nutritional Therapist and Clinical Nutrition. By chance, his tutor was working on Harley Street at the Centre of Nutritional Medicine, looking after a load of rugby players from Saracens (a top UK rugby team). The players did so well that Matt and his tutor got their work expanded to look after the England national players. That was three years before the World Cup

'We got the jump on the other international teams as we were ahead of our time, and became the 2003 Rugby World Champions.'

I asked Matt what separates the best in a high-performance environment where everyone is driven, everyone is talented?

'A lot of it comes down to what you eat, how you hydrate, and then what supplementation you use. Nutrition is important on all levels, not just for the elite athlete.'

In our conversation, we kept coming back to bringing balance to the body. The way you excel in sport is by creating a severe state of imbalance in the body by training and playing the sport at a high level. This will completely deplete reserves and destroy tissue.

'The quicker the human can return to what's called homeostasis, or rebalance those systems, the better. We have the capacity when we replenish and repair properly to rebuild at a slightly higher capacity than we were before. It's all about how quickly you can adapt and recover between training sessions. On a very simple level, you're looking at energy balance, so you're looking at the right kind of macro-nutrient ratio – proteins, fats, carbohydrates, replenishing the carbohydrate reserve rapidly, but not in a way which is going to increase insulin resistance.'

All Matt's protocols begin by making someone insulin sensitive, or helping them utilise their carbohydrates in the most efficient manner possible. That includes obvious stuff like stripping out all processed foods, which is always my first port of call if I am dealing with anyone (including myself) looking to step things up. Getting the simple things right is where the initial and large improvements are – if it's in a plastic wrapper, don't eat it.

For the man who wants to manage his energy better, this is the key advice Matt gives as a starting point:

'Ninety-nine per cent of the people I see don't track their food intake and they don't track their energy expenditure. Before you come to a nutritionist with any problems, do those two things and you'll probably work out 75% of it on your own.'

Another useful tactic Matt shares is to monitor the quantity and quality of your sleep.

'Not everyone responds well to magnesium supplementation, it can affect your sleep. Tracking your sleep arms you with that data. Also, I know if I have had a high percentage of quality sleep the night before, I'll get better performance on those days.'

With that sort of data, you can go at it in your training or hold back accordingly. As with everything in this book, applied knowledge is power.

ARE YOU HUNGRY?

For the last four years, I have been consistently applying intermittent fasting as a foundation for my nutrition. Obviously, what you eat plays a major role in how you perform, but I am going to focus here on the timing, the brief rationale behind intermittent fasting, the extreme application, and what I have actually been doing long term.

I really got into intermittent fasting after interviewing John Romaniello, author of *Engineering the Alpha*, who talked about applying the 16/8 fasting protocol made popular by Martin Berkhan. Essentially, it is eating within an eight-hour window and fasting for the remaining sixteen hours of the day and night, taking in less food (fewer calories) and carbohydrates on rest days, while protein intake remains high on all days. There is a little more to it, which is just one Google search away, but that is the core of it.

I'll now whip through why you may choose to try intermittent fasting and what I have experienced. Generally, you'll be hungry less often, and as you're eating less often, it's easier to consume fewer calories. You can lose unwanted fat while maintaining or increasing muscle, depending on your training regime.

The hormonal benefits are increased insulin sensitivity and increased human growth hormone to help deal with cortisone (stress hormone), which has also been linked to belly fat. Longer fasts can encourage cellular repair which helps with disease prevention and aging.

Typically, everyone already fasts for six to ten hours overnight when they sleep. That's why the first food intake of the day is called 'breakfast'. Intermittent fasting is just about extending that natural fast.

I started with 16/8, as I suggest you do (if you're curious), and I revert back to that level as and when I feel I need to. The majority of the time, I operate with a fourteen- to fifteen-hour fast, and the worst-case scenario is twelve hours fasting (which is barely a fast once you have learned to live like this). When I'm 'on it', I do a twenty-four to thirty-six-hour fast once a month.

It's not for everyone, but this is why I like it in addition to the benefits I've already mentioned. No matter what else happens – if you're travelling, have limited options or are making poor food choices – fasting is a core strategy you can still maintain control of among all of this. The eating window is flexible; the fasting can begin and stop when I decide. I can move the window for special family breakfasts, late dinners or even drunken 2am feasts.

Usually, my fasts are from 8pm to 10 or 11am, but you may find eating later in the night or stopping earlier works for you. Longer fasts of twenty-four hours or more are usually preceded by a 'feast' day which is a great mental break, but I only follow the feast/fast protocol if I am restricting overall calories and following a strict 16/8 timeline.

Fasting is a good challenge, enhancing resilience and hormonal optimisation. I like the discipline, the power of control, and being the opposite of a 'hangry' person who has to eat every five minutes.

ACTION 18: ENERGY CURRENT

- On a scale of one to ten, how energetic do/did you feel today?
- How active were you today?
- How many hours of sleep did you get last night?
- When was the last time you slept for eight hours?
- When was the last time you trained for thirty minutes or more?
- When was the last time you did some fun exercise?
- What was the duration of your last overnight fast?
- When was the last time you think you went sixteen or more hours without eating?
- Did you eat something out of a plastic wrapper today? How many things?
- How much water did you drink today?
- When was the last time you did something you consider 'meditational'?
- Did you take any supplementation today? If so, what?

This is your reality now, so what would you like it to be? What do you think it would take for you to operate with more energy in life? Do your current actions match your intentions for your energy?

MOOLA

'You must gain control over your money or
the lack of it will forever control you.'

DAVE RAMSEY, AUTHOR *FINANCIAL PEACE*

THE TWO SPEARS OF GOLD

'Moola' is a British slang term for money. One of the basic masculine concepts in life is to provide for and protect your family, and money is one of the essential tools to achieve this.

The Chinese character for money has three pieces to it. One is gold and the other symbols are two spears. Why are two spears in the character? In my mind, it's because there are two different purposes of money: to survive and to thrive. This dual nature of money is why people have such strong and different experiences with it. The two spears actually represent the outward struggle for survival and the battle to be fought within.

The majority of men are just fighting the outward battle to provide for themselves and their family. Fewer fight the inward battle, which is where the real riches are to be won and lost.

For years, I didn't focus on money so long as I was surviving. I was doing OK and my interests were elsewhere. I definitely did not focus on the inward game, which was the reason why my outward game was distinctly average. Through my upbringing, society and environment, I had been subtly and, in many cases, not so subtly fed what I'll now call propaganda about anyone who thrives financially: 'If you have a lot of money, you very likely have questionable morals, you value money over people, you sacrifice health or family or both for money, and are pretty much a dick.'

With these thoughts hiding in my subconscious mind, would I ever aspire to do well financially? To alienate friends, family and be greedy? Of course I wouldn't. No one aspires to be a dick; it just happens along the way.

Many of my early decisions were affected by this story I had accepted. I dismissed professions if I believed they earned too much. Throughout my twenties, I loved the start-up, the ascension, the underdog mentality, but when things started to go well, I'd pull the plug, always having my plan B, my safety net, there for comfort.

Weird as that sounds, at the time it was quite natural, and looking back, I can understand why I would do that. To thrive financially, you must first win the battle within or all other efforts will be undermined.

'... whether that's inherited imprint from your parents, something that's passed on to you, you shouldn't be having to struggle with. It could be poverty consciousness, where you have a ceiling on your income and you don't know how to get past that.'

TOBY ALEXANDER, COACH AND HEALING FACILITATOR

THE RICH ARSEHOLE AND THE POOR ARSEHOLE

Poverty is more a state of mind than it is an outward condition. If you feel like you don't have enough money, how much would it take for you to feel OK? Would you be stuck with this feeling no matter what? What are you doing to change your circumstances, or are you too busy embracing the badge of 'poor' as it must mean you're a nice person, right?

My own issues finally started to change (it was a slow process) when I was meeting more and more financially successful people. Guess what – they (generally) were not arseholes. Amazing! Well, it was ground-breaking to me, thanks to my upbringing coupled with how the media paints anyone with money as a bit of a villain. I finally realised this was just a story I had held on to for too long.

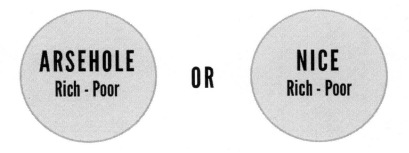

ARSEHOLE
Rich - Poor

OR

NICE
Rich - Poor

Don't assign an attitude to a number in a bank. People only discredit the achievements of others when they don't want to shine the light closer to home. Self-worth is a big player here – if you don't believe you are worthy of the finer things in life or the freedom money can bring, then the universe tends to agree with you. It is all about having an impact, solving a problem for a fair exchange of value. You must have a powerful sense of your own worth and be able to put it out there. This comes back to taking action – you must first have done something that is worthy of your own respect.

The reality is that most of us are currently where we deserve to be financially. We could all earn more right now, but what would our perceived sacrifices be? If we think they are too great, we won't take the actions. You are where you are today financially because of you, is a powerful concept to claim. Until you can truly grasp this, how can you expect to change it for the better? So many people waste so much time blaming fate for their situation. Winning the internal money battle can mean the difference between being financially down in the dumps and flying high. It's that simple.

ACTION 19: MONEY TRIPOD

Repeat the tripod process from Part I, but now make all three limiting 'I will never...' statements about your finances.

MAKE YOUR MONEY MATTER

COLE HATTER, USA

'The truth is that you can spend your life
any way you want, but you can spend it only once.'

JOHN C. MAXWELL, AUTHOR OF *THE 21 IRREFUTABLE LAWS OF LEADERSHIP*

Cole is a serial entrepreneur. He has built several multi-million-dollar businesses and he is all about making money matter. When I asked, 'Are you ready to *Awaken Your Alpha* today?' as I always do to set the tone for my guests, his answer made me smile.

'I stay ready so I ain't gotta get ready. I'm a dad and a husband and that's it man. They're the most important to me. Two daughters, a wife and two girl dogs, so it's nothing but estrogen up in here! Awaken your alpha I definitely can resonate with because I'm drowning in estrogen.'

Originally from Orange County, California, Cole took evening and weekend classes while in high school so that when he graduated, he could go into the fire service. His 'awakening' when everything changed happened when he was twenty-one years old, driving with his two best friends to Vegas.

'We got in a rollover car accident and two of us were ejected. Matt, who was not ejected, was rushed to the hospital in an ambulance. Steve and I, who were ejected, got rushed to the hospital in a helicopter because we had life-threatening injuries. The long and short of that is that Matt and I survived, and Steve didn't. So that rocked my world because not only had I just been in a near-death experience, but I lost my best friend in that experience. I had the grief of losing him and the guilt of surviving.'

Fast forward two months. Cole and Matt, the other survivor from the car accident, fell into a mine shaft together. Cole made it out and Matt didn't.

Cole lost his two most important friends in accidents he was involved in. In the aftermath, having to recover physically and mentally, he turned towards entrepreneurship.

'That's what gave me this fire in my butt to make my life matter. All of us know life is precious. We all have lost somebody, a friend, a grandparent, somebody in our lives, and we think that we get 80 to 100 years on this earth. That's until both your twenty-one-year-old best friends die.'

Cole told me he'd had this in his mind:

'I'm going to be successful. I'm going to get serious about my life…later. I'm young.'

The average twenty-one-year-old guy is in 'party boy' mode. Cole was heading to Vegas, I was heading to Ibiza at that age. We all think we have more time. I'm sure Cole's buddies thought they had plenty of time to do their 'things'. Unfortunately, this mentality can continue throughout your life, regardless of your age.

To start with, Cole went into business with his father. They raised money, started buying and selling real estate, and it worked phenomenally. Looking back now, he describes it as good timing. The 2008 recession taught him a brutal lesson: that he didn't actually know how to invest in real estate. He was losing money hand over fist and it was the cheapest option to quit the business. He moved to Mexico for seven months, working full time with a non-profit organisation building houses for homeless families.

'I end up starting an orphanage down there that I still have to this day. I saw that even though I wasn't making any active money, the little bit that I had left from my days of business could go so far in helping people. I was like, "This is insane."

'That first three years in my real estate business I would have six-figure months on occasion. So, I was balling for a twenty-two-year-old. That was twenty-two to twenty-five years, and it was all gone. Now I've moved to Mexico, I'm twenty-six years old and a few hundred bucks could feed orphans where before I was spending $3,000 a month on just car payments. I felt a little bit embarrassed that when I had money, I spent it all on myself, and now that I had to sell all that crap because I lost my income, I had nothing to show for it.'

Cole became obsessed with the idea of making money matter. He found that spending his own money where he got to witness it feeding children was far more fulfilling and ultimately addictive than giving to charity. It then became part of his lifestyle.

Cole came back to the United States and went on to make millions of dollars in real estate again, designing the 'for purpose business model' for his new companies instead of starting a non-profit and having to raise money. A business that's a self-sustaining ecosystem can pay for its own bills and initiatives.

'People say you can't buy happiness. That's baloney. Try buying a starving child's food. When you see them eat and you see their eyes looking at you as they're feeding themselves, if that doesn't make you happy, you need to check your pulse.'

ACTION 20: DOUGH DIAGNOSIS

Money is such a vast subject, and many books are dedicated just to this subject. In my experience, they all share one common theme as a priority: you have to know what you're shooting for. Make it specific to you. Take some space and time to lay out all the accurate figures.

This is a good exercise to do with or without a partner. Answer the following questions:

- What is your own definition of financial freedom?
- How much will that cost?
- What amount do you need to cover your current essential living needs per month?
- What amount do you need to cover your lifestyle wants per month?
- What amount would you like to invest in your future, and how?
- What amount or percentage of your earnings would you like to give back? List some ways that mean something to you. Time is also a valuable asset to give.

When I was interviewing JV Crum III, Author of *Conscious Millionaire*, he identified some vital habits to get a handle on. I have included these habits and the following exercise from his bestselling book. Use them as a starting point to assess if your financial habits are making or breaking you, and then to get back on point.

- Spend less than you make
- Live on a budget
- Save at least 10%

- Maintain an emergency fund
- Give back regularly
- Pay cash for depreciating assets (excluding big ticket items such as a house)
- If you use one, pay off credit cards each statement (if you can't pay for it in thirty days, don't buy it)

ACTION 21: MONEY MODE

Identify which habits from the above list you want to start or improve on. What is one habit that you will take action on in the next twenty-four hours? What is that action?

Write an action you could do to develop each of these habits.

Tony Robbins covers financial ascension well in *Money Master the Game,* when he talks about the different levels of financial dreams: first the basics, then the lifestyle, then increasing freedom for you and your family to choose. Individual power comes from working out what level is genuinely significant to you, what your numbers are, and why they are meaningful to you. For most men, money musts (when we get down to numbers) are very different. When you know your numbers, financial freedom is likely more achievable than you currently believe. It is also worth taking note that when we think, I have money issues, it is more likely we have a fulfilment issue.

SUMMARY

'Action may not always bring happiness, but
there is no happiness without action.'

BENJAMIN DISRAELI, FORMER BRITISH PRIME MINISTER

- Great tactics are still just tactics. The power comes in consistent and effective execution.

- Assuming you are going to die when you're old with plenty of warning to be able to tick things off your bucket list makes you a donut. Don't be a donut.

- Limiting beliefs can ruin your happiness. Do the work to identify, discredit and replace these beliefs with ones that empower you.

- Experiment and choose habits that leave you more resilient to depression. Take a proactive stance on your mental health and have some kind of routine for when it starts to go south.

- Go on the hunt for, and within, your opportunities.

- How you manage your energy will dictate what you are able to experience in this life.

- Know your numbers and why you are pursuing a certain amount of money. Work on your inner game as well as developing your outer game to move you towards financial fulfilment.

ACT III

ASCENSION

'Our destiny is not determined by the
number of times we stumble, but by
the number of times we rise up,
dust ourselves off and move forward.'

DIETER F UCHTDORF, GERMAN AVIATOR

I will be breaking 'Ascension' down into:

ASSOCIATE

ARENA

ACHIEVE

ADVENTURE

In this section, you will:

- Become the man you want to be, through how you act and who you hang out with
- Do what you must to up your game, cutting out toxic relationships and interactions
- Develop your presence and ability to communicate powerfully
- Identify key areas to increase control of your state and your power
- Gain tactics to reduce stress and feeling overwhelmed
- Decide on adventures that fire you up
- Do things worthy of your own respect and think about aligning with others on a similar mission (who do you need to start reaching out to?)

THE LAST OF MAN'S FREEDOMS

'The way of warrior skill is the way of nature.
When you are in line with the power of nature,
knowing the rhythm of all situations, you will be
able to cut and strike the enemy naturally.'

MIYAMOTO MUSASHI, SIXTEENTH CENTURY JAPANESE SWORD MASTER

The Samurai handles his weapon as we should handle our daily tasks. Your enemy is resistance, whatever form that takes for you on any given day. Mental strength is essential to handle the day-to-day work that must be done to achieve greatness over the years that make up your life.

Ascension is not about looking down on others who have made decisions in life that don't serve them. It's about you continuing to rise up internally and externally through your path. It's about adjusting the setting of your 'life thermostat' to what you are capable of. It is an approach to life; an attitude; something you bring about each and every day through your decisions; the mindset to look after yourself and those around you, physically and mentally, with no regrets or holding back out of fear.

The last of man's freedoms that can be taken is the ability to choose your own attitude in any situation, and ultimately your own way to deal with it. This is a concept identified by Viktor E Frankl in a book I highly recommend, *Man's Search for Meaning*. In the most horrific circumstances of the Nazi death camps, in a situation where people had been stripped of everything, this was what life and death came down to: how do you choose to deal with your life?

Focus on your strengths without sacrificing a core aspect of your life for success in another. This is why this book's framework is powerful: it highlights and places importance on essential components to thrive as a man, whatever your chosen path. We must have this level of awareness to avoid burnout and missing some of life's greatest moments.

ACTION 22: RECOVERY

I have recovery blocks in my day, week, month and year. As much as I like to think it sometimes, I am not a machine, and neither are you. Whether it's meditation, entertainment, wandering, socialising, random offline days, or a night away, be tactical and live proactively to create space.

What are three or more activities you could use to 'de-load'? Think daily, weekly, monthly and more. Where and at what times will they be most beneficial to you? Get them locked in now on your schedule and calendar.

ASSOCIATE

'Don't ever stop or let the world's negativity disenchant you or your spirit. If you surround yourself with love and the right people, anything is possible.'

ADAM GREEN, SINGER-SONGWRITER AND FILM-MAKER

HIGHEST PROBABILITY OF THE DEEPEST IMPACT

Of all the things I've mentioned in this book, who you associate with, who you align with and spend your time with, will have the highest probability of the deepest impact. This can be as negatively powerful as it can be positive in your life, so take a look at who you spend your time with. Do they suck the life out of a room or do they light it up? Is their default mode to complain and criticise others, or one of excitement, celebrating others' achievements? Do you leave after spending time with them feeling positive or negative?

Quite simply, I avoid negative people like the plague. The only energy they get from me is the energy I invest in getting away from them, quickly.

Don't leave meeting the right people to chance. Be proactive. The world is now a small place where you can connect with like-minded people and choose the company you keep – your own alpha alliance. Knowing a person's purpose and mission is a great place to start.

For example, my mission with *Awaken Your Alpha*, the podcast, the book and my Mastermind Alliance, is: 'Practices that increase awareness to make decisive daily actions to progress, perform and thrive as a man, aligning with others on a similar mission.' The 'Mastermind Alliance' concept was first described by Napoleon Hill almost eighty years ago in his book *Think and Grow Rich*:

> 'The coordination of knowledge and effort between two or more people who work towards a definite purpose in a spirit of harmony.'

The increased energy created by the alliance becomes available to everyone in the group. This concept was inspired by Hill's many conversations over a twenty-year period with financially successful men like Henry Ford, Thomas Edison, and Andrew Carnegie, who attributed his entire fortune and success to his mastermind group.

ACTION 23: ALIGN

Become the man you want to be now. How would that guy need to be, to act, to achieve your vision? Who would he hang out with? Who would he not hang out with? If you associated yourself with that group now, would your presence stand out like a sore thumb or would you be able to hold your own and continue to rise up?

Do what you need to do to make the changes. Take the steps and invest in yourself.

Who do you need to start reaching out to?

DEVELOP YOUR PRESENCE

DAVID SHEPARD, UK

'You are more powerful than
you think you are. Act accordingly.'

SETH GODIN, AUTHOR OF *PURPLE COW*

Your ability to communicate, to have presence, impacts every aspect of your life. One of my favourite examples of this is Englishman David Shepard.

David has spent well over 10,000 hours on NLP. He's the trainers' trainer, who has worked with countless celebrities and high-level politicians. When I first saw David speak, I was hit by how everyone was so engaged and relaxed while listening to his story. In short, he had presence.

If someone is telling an interesting story, regardless of who they are, you'll want to know the end. It's human nature. I especially liked the way David would start a few stories, all strategic, then finish each depending on the point he wanted to make. This is what great movies do, too: they open storylines, but don't finish them straight away. It's such a powerful technique when it's done right, and one to keep in mind when you're planning to present yourself.

'NLP is the difference that makes a difference.'

Some people are 'naturals': natural performers; natural presenters; natural salespeople; natural parents. They're just born with the skill. Is David one of them? No. According to him, he is not a natural-born anything.

The creators of NLP, Richard Bandler and John Grinder, described it as 'an attitude and a methodology that leaves behind a trail of techniques'. NLP is about saying to ourselves, 'This person is a natural. What are they doing to make them so? What do they do with their body? What is the structure of their thinking? How do they communicate using their voice?', then being able to model that in ourselves or other people. When we start thinking the same way, structuring our words in the same way, we get the same results.

Before David discovered NLP, his first business had failed:

> 'I didn't have the belief that I could sell or do. With NLP, I changed all of that.'

Everyone is selling something. It could just be an idea, like my podcast, for example. If the men featured in this book didn't think the podcast was worth any value, they wouldn't have been a guest on it. It may just be you trying to convince your mates which one is the best pub to go to or movie to watch.

I find it really inspiring that in his own words, David says he is not a natural-born anything. So many people who are 'natural' can't explain how to do what they do; it's described as 'charisma'. But you can study charismatic people and emulate what they do. I used that approach when preparing for my TEDx talk. It's inspiring to know that you can learn how to have more presence.

NLP is a huge topic in itself, but one of the fundamentals that will instil confidence and belief to build your presence on is the ability to get your message across.

ACTION 24: INCIDENT–POINT–BENEFIT

This is an exercise about being clear and effective with your message, taken from David Shepard and Tad James's book *Presenting Magically*. Once you have planned points one to three below, you have one minute to tell your story. Tell it aloud while standing up.

- **Incident.** Write down a brief story that happened to you or something you heard. It can be anything, but there has to be a point you want to get across
- **Point.** What is the point? 'And the point of this is...'
- **Benefit.** Finally, it's important to clarify the benefit to your audience (not you) of understanding that point. 'And the benefit to you is...'

When you are nervous about communicating or presenting to an audience, whether it's to one or many, it is easy to ramble on for half an hour and not make many (if any) clear points. If you can manage to convey a clear story, point and benefit in one minute, in theory you will be capable of conveying thirty in half an hour.

The exercise above backs up another key strategy I used for my TEDx talk. In his bestselling book *Talk Like TED*, Carmine Gallo analysed Brian Stevenson's talk, which had one of the longest standing ovations and is considered one of the most persuasive TED talks ever, categorising what Brian said into logos, ethos, and pathos. These are the three components that Aristotle believed must be present for persuasion to occur. Logos is basically logic, data and statistics; ethos is anything that establishes credibility; and pathos is anything appealing to emotions, eg a story. Carmine Gallo's findings were that the ideal proportions for persuasion were 25% logos, 10% ethos, and 65% – by far the most important component – storytelling (pathos).

The three components, and more importantly the ratio of logos, ethos and pathos, are crucial when you want to get your message heard in any situation. You may be charismatic, but if you are way off on one of these fundamental components, you will never be as effective or impactful as you could have been.

Before stepping on to the TEDx stage, I ran my talk through this same analysis several times and tweaked it to make sure I was confident in my ratios. I ended up with roughly 60% stories (pathos), 25% logic (logos) and 15% credibility (ethos) to get my message across (search *TEDx Adam Lewis Walker* to see the result). Any presentations or scenarios you are able review that either went well or shockingly badly, run them through the logos, ethos, pathos filter and the results will give you insights as to why.

AUTHENTIC ATTRACTION

'The truthful inside story of almost any man's life – if told modestly and without offending egotism – is most entertaining.'

DALE CARNEGIE, AUTHOR OF
HOW TO WIN FRIENDS AND INFLUENCE PEOPLE

It is essential to be confident and authentic in who you are. In addition to speaking, I believe this rings true for life as a whole. Many men think they've got to be somebody else, that they aren't personally good enough. When they speak or present, all of a sudden, it's like they switch to being a different person.

Even if they're really good, straight away, this brings questions to my mind. Why are they being different? Why do they have to switch? Are they not the same person I was talking to five minutes before? Why are they not being themselves? What are they hiding?

If you were to meet me in the street after listening to my podcasts, to some extent, you would already know my essence, and you would find me 'as is'. The great thing is, that means I can relax, be myself. If you do or don't like me, I am OK with that. It is your choice.

There is no point pretending to be someone else in an attempt to please others. No one will really know who you are (including yourself) if you do. You can't put a 'front' on long term and be happy. David Shepard speaks to an audience of some size 200 days a year. Imagine doing that with a 'front' – he'd be burnt out.

> 'When I walk out on stage, whether it's in front of five people
> or five thousand people, I am me.'

It's this key belief that David has, that is the cornerstone of an alpha male. When we're being who we are, we attract what we desire in our lives. All of us have way more ability, more skill than we believe we have. It's when we're trying to pretend we're someone else that we attract all kinds of non-desirable things.

> 'There is no such thing as an un-resourceful person, just un-resourceful states. What happens is they go into this emotional state that doesn't enable them to tap into that genius. Whatever anybody is doing – speaking, presenting, selling, their relationship or whatever – we all have doubts. We all have fears, we all have limiting beliefs. In the moment, what you need to do is think. How do I want to be? Then act as if you're that person. Act as if you can do it.

Pretend you can do it. You know, sometimes you pretend so well you fool yourself, and that's a real life skill.'

There are techniques that enable you to do that, even if you have a phobia of public speaking. Then the most important thing becomes the state you're in. For speaking, being relaxed and comfortable is the benchmark; for other arenas and individuals, it may vary slightly.

I asked former UFC fighter Charlie 'The Spaniard' Brenneman to explain what being inside the cage and having to perform is like.

'I liken it to an airplane. You put on your safety belt, they take off, you pray it all goes well, but it's up to the universe. A fight is kind of that way, you know, when you get in the octagon and Bruce pops up, looks at you and says, "Ready, fight!" It's like you're kind of out of body. It's back to instinct and you're going with it. You've done all the work, you have just got to do what you can do and go for it.'

Many high performers talk about an out-of-body experience and being in the zone, which is basically your optimal state to perform. When Charlie fought Rick Story in his famous underdog victory, he was totally in his zone.

'I almost turn off my conscious mind and I just trust my gut. That's when I perform my best. When I look at other fights where I was very mechanical, over thinking, then I got knocked or choked out.'

When you have put in the work, done everything within your power to prepare, and it is time to perform, just do it. Earn the right to trust your gut, then develop your ability to control the state you are in to perform.

ACTION 25: MOMENT IN THE ZONE

Think of a time you accomplished something that made you feel incredible; a time you felt empowered, confident, full of energy, that you could do anything you put your mind to.

Refine it. What was the most powerful part of being you in that zone? Imagine a second or two of video replaying it for you to watch. Notice every little detail.

Attach... a meaning to it. Why is that moment so significant to you?

Physiology. How did you feel physically in that moment? How did you stand, breathe? What did you hear?

Stand up. Close your eyes and experience all of the above again. Take a slightly difference stance, if that makes sense. Pinch and hold one of your wrists, build up a little bounce, release your wrist, drop into a 'ready' stance with a deep 'Huhhh!'

The last bit sounds nuts on paper, but you have to experience it.

There are so many versions of state control and anchoring out there. This specific one I experienced via top entrepreneur Nick Unsworth at an event of his, after I'd interviewed him on the podcast.

What you keep in your mind determines how you feel. How you feel affects your physiology, and your physiology affects the way you feel. I like to keep this top of mind. Choose your methods of state control and change the way you feel whenever you want.

INCREASE YOUR FREQUENCY

TOBY ALEXANDER, USA

This brings me to my intense conversation with Toby Alexander, who is known as a leading authority in the areas of human behaviour, DNA activation and ascension. He works with people who want to attain something in their lives that they currently do not have (happiness, inner peace, financial independence or a soul mate) to clear the source of their blockages.

'Whatever alpha wants, alpha gets.'

When Toby said this in our interview, straight away I thought of the Law of Deservedness. This law states that you will only manifest into your life what you feel you deserve at a subconscious level. And if you manifest more, you will either sabotage it or push it away.

There are few true alphas in the world. We do have a lot of fake alphas, though, coming from a place of low self-esteem and trying to amp themselves up.

'To become a spiritual alpha, it is to become a real, whole man who is completely elegant in his speech, who treats others with kindness, but who also embodies that solid, grounded power.'

Toby grew up in Texas which he describes as an alpha state – very competitive. He worked his whole way through college on a chain gang with three other guys, hammering spikes and levelling railroad tracks in 100 degrees Fahrenheit all day long. Toby got to hear all the other guys' stories, all the mistakes they had made and the advice they had to give. Every time he finished working with them, he headed back to college with more enthusiasm to master what he wanted to do in life.

'I've always been inspired by challenges. I'm constantly challenging myself. That's really what drives me: human performance. And that's what led me to studying about the human DNA.'

Toby kept comparing people to computers' operating systems, and that made a lot of sense to me. If you want to make changes, you cannot simply open up a Word document and say, 'OK, now my PC is a Mac with no susceptibility to viruses.'

'If we don't work at the subconscious quantum level [small, sudden, significant] we're going to work at the conscious mind level where I'm talking to you and there is no permanent transformation.'

You can say things, but until you believe them on a subconscious level, you will sabotage yourself without even being aware that you're doing it. In this sense, you will keep going around in a loop until you address some of your deep-rooted values and beliefs to align them with what you really want in life.

'It's like the BIOS [Basic Input Output System] of your computer. Your BIOS has everything that has happened [to you], and mostly things that happened from birth until age seven where your mind was completely open to all kinds of suggestions. You need to go to the root of that specific twisted energy pattern at the quantum level of the person and transmute [transform] that by bringing in the exact opposite frequency. When you do that, then you're working at the quantum level which then projects out in all areas of your life. Your frequency rises, and you attract a whole new grid of people, places, times, things and events.'

In Indian thought, *chakras* are the centres of spiritual power in the human body. Your heart is one of these and represents your soul identity. Toby believes most people are never able to access their higher consciousness or awareness because the DNA that controls them is turned off.

Toby told me he has the ability to 'read' people within five minutes, so obviously I offered myself up as a guinea pig for this exercise.

'I read people's soul record to determine what are your innate gifts, your talents. What are the specific things that you're bringing in here as something that you can express abundantly? For example, just reading you right now, I can tell that your primary energy is something called divine self-expression. A person with divine self-expression is very gifted with being able to get information out to others. Your gifts will spontaneously come out while you're speaking. So, you could be talking to me or giving me a coaching call and you would be able to pull in information without even knowing where it came from to help me.'

So I have divine self-expression, but how much am I using it? Likely only a certain percentage. What are the blockages to me being able to fully embody my divine self-expression? What are the blockages to you accessing your higher awareness? When you fully embody it in every single moment, you cannot help but be massively abundant.

Toby collects high-quality Montblanc journals and pens. He is focused on everything around him being the best as everything has a frequency. When you use the best pen available to write, for example, you are actually setting your best self in motion. It's an intention. The other extreme would be writing your journal or your notes with a kid's crayon on a scrap of paper. I kept this in mind with the environments and instruments I chose to write this book.

'Everything you do is either making you stronger, making you more of an alpha, or making you weaker. When you find out what those things are [that make you stronger], you focus on that and you get stronger. Your life just flows.'

We discussed what holds men back from operating on a higher level, from increasing their frequency, and why that is significant. It came down to this: it's not what you do or what you study, it's who you are. Your frequency attracts you to the exact frequency of people and opportunities around you. The higher the frequency you have, the higher the frequency of the people you're going to attract in your life.

'If you and I were not a similar frequency, we wouldn't be having this conversation right now. So, my whole focus was clearing the blockages that I inherited from my parents of lack, limitation – you know, beliefs that are not good enough.'

What do you need to increase your frequency on?

ARENA

'When I let go of what I am, I become what I might be.'

LAO TZU, FOUNDER OF TAOISM

You create your arena, your environment. Not just your physical environment, but as importantly, your mental environment. Your personal code and philosophy will go a long way towards doing this.

People will put a lot of energy into telling you why they cannot do something because of their environment. Take ownership of yours, creating one that supports your vision, your 'training ground' for higher performance, wherever you are now.

If you feel you don't have much to build your environment on, think of the *Rocky* movies. Celebrate and make the most of what you do have. Metaphorically beat the crap out of meat hanging in the freezer or scramble up a snow-covered mountain to be the man you want to be. I am constantly in training, and one of my favourite t-shirts says '*Winners Train, Losers Complain*', which is pretty self-explanatory.

A PODCAST FOR CHANGE

At the end of 2013, I was still teaching part time at a college just south of London. It was a pretty comfy job, and that made me uncomfortable. My current environment was not supporting my move to the United States; it was not supporting who I had to become to live out there. I needed to change my current actions if I was to get there.

Against advice, I decided to quit my last job and start the *Awaken Your Alpha* podcast. I had been caught in limbo for too long, deciding whether to be an employee or entrepreneur; I was now fully committed as an entrepreneur and I dived in headfirst.

Within a month, I had launched the podcast, which ended up coming out the same week as *The Tim Ferriss Show*. Tim is the author of *The 4-Hour Work Week* which was one of my first really inspirational reads a decade ago. I was up against it, but hit the number one spot on iTunes for my categories within the first week. I took the screen shots early, as when America woke up hours after the UK, Tim would knock me off the top spot.

I didn't know exactly what I would do with all this, but I was now headed in the right direction. My environment and my arena had definitely shifted, even though my physical location was the same for the time being. I was becoming the man I needed to be to live the life I envisioned for the near future.

Make no mistake, your current environment will not dictate your future if you don't let it. With a vision and daily action to get there, both physically and mentally, you will not be where you are now for long. History is littered with greats who have applied this principle. There is always someone who has awakened their alpha from more challenging circumstances than yours or mine. This is the fight for your life, so think about what tough decisions you must make to change your arena.

DETOX TIMELINE

With a clear code in place that supports your vision, you will soon discover things, situations and people in your life that are particularly toxic to you and your continued efforts to grow. If your why is strong enough, rise up and detox now. Don't waste your energy complaining about people and situations; take responsibility for your involvement in allowing negativity to happen in your arena repeatedly and predictably, then take steps to change today. You can be standing in a pile of crap looking up at the blue sky and walking out of it, or you can be staring down, focusing on the crap as you continue to stand in it. Your call.

> 'You have to be willing to murder who
> you were yesterday in order to change.
> It's a brutal process.'
>
> **CAMERON GALLAGHER**

There may be some stuff in your life that is clearly negative, so start your change there. However, when we are talking about high performance, sometimes it is less obvious. Life is an experiment; you have to do different things to get a better result. Sometimes your environment can change really quickly, but you still get to decide your attitude in any situation – whether to re-commit to thrive or become a victim of circumstance.

ACTION 26: TOXIC LIST

Physically – what locations/people are you going to stop being around?

Mentally – what do you need to stop consuming/talking about?

Situations – what activities/groups/scenarios do you need to avoid?

ENVIRONMENT REVOLUTION

RAMY ROMANY, EGYPT

A good friend of mine is cinematographer and director Ramy Romany, who's had four Emmy Award wins and nine nominations, and most importantly (to me) he's worked with Arnold Schwarzenegger.

Originally from Egypt, Ramy now lives in Los Angeles. We have hung out a few times, and when I heard his story, I was hooked. It sounded more like a movie than real life, and I knew I had to share it in this book.

Ramy was born into a documentary-filmmaking family. His name was on the rolling credits of BBC and National Geographic documentaries when he was eleven and twelve years old, working next to some of the world's best documentary filmmakers, and it all took off from there.

Ramy left Egypt on 30 January 2011. The previous day, his dream had been to live in Egypt for the rest of his life and grow his empire.

His wife Sharra, who was also a cameraperson, had actually left Los Angeles to live in Egypt, but things all changed when the Egyptian Revolution began on 25 January 2011.

> 'I grew up in Egypt and I knew how safe and secure Egypt is. I looked at it [the revolution] on the news and I thought it was just a couple of kids on the streets and everything is going to be fine. Everyone that was really passionate about it couldn't get their newsfeed from the TV as TV was lying; TV is government. They only got the newsfeed from Twitter. The police decided to shut Twitter and Facebook down in Egypt. That's when they made their biggest mistake.'

As people couldn't access their newsfeed, they headed out on to the streets to see what was actually happening. The revolution came into full effect when there were millions and millions of people on the streets from every city in Egypt.

> 'That night it got so crazy, and the police decided, "OK, you don't like the police, we'll show you what it will be like without us."'

The police decided to abandon the country. Instantly, Egypt was converted into a crazy, lawless land where prisoners, including terrorists, were free on the streets. Ramy started hearing artillery fire around his house. He lived on 16 acres in a gated community, and he saw people jumping the fences of the houses. The criminals were taking over.

The American Embassy then called his wife and told her to leave, now. Things were going to get bad. It was late, so Ramy and his family had to spend the night in their food storage room.

> 'We boiled sand and oil just in case anyone tried to climb in. In my head, I'm just thinking I have to protect my wife;

I have to protect my six-month-old baby. That's it. That's all I can think.

'The next morning, we take our car, we drive straight to the airport hoping to get out, and that drive was a scene from a movie to say the least. It looked like the end of the world. There's kids with guns, kids with swords, and people getting killed on the street. Tanks on the street to protect government structures as their main objective. We're hearing on the radio that kids are stopping people next to their neighbourhoods to try to protect their neighbourhoods. They are young kids, they act first. They have killed so many innocent people in their cars because they suspect them. I decided not to stop for anyone. I'm going to just keep going to the airport. I decided it's time to murder a human being if I need to.

'At the end of the road, kids are trying to stop my car. I am thinking of that kid under my car, letting my feet step on the gas and not on the brakes. I will keep going. I'll hear his skull shudder under my car, but I'll keep going. I will defend my family. I would never think of murdering another human being, but I was ready. As I approached them, I was staring right in his eye, pressing the gas, and I knew it was the right thing to do. Just before he actually goes under my car, he hits the top of my car, and luckily I did not kill that kid.'

Ramy drove straight to the airport. With his daughter Sophia strapped to his chest, he and his wife ran, trying to get on any plane. There was one plane that 'should' get out with two seats left on it and they got the seats, but couldn't get inside the airport. Everyone was stuck.

However, as part of his job was getting equipment through customs, Ramy knew who to bribe to get behind the lines. They ended up being the first people on that plane… but no planes were leaving.

'The plane is not full and most of the crew can't make it. We feel like someone is going to come up and say we're de-boarding the plane, we're not going to take off. All of a sudden, the pilot decides to close the door and takes off.'

They made it to New York, not realising they would never return to their home.

How would you cope in Ramy's situation? How would you adapt, transferring your skills and starting from scratch in a new environment? Obviously, this is an extreme example, but the point is that however tough your current environment is, it will not dictate your outcome. Your attitude will.

I found Ramy's attitude to be something we can all learn from in our daily lives.

'We started a new life here in Los Angeles where my wife lived in the first place. Once the work permit arrived, I went out. I'm ready to do my cinematography… and I'm extremely talented. I'm ready for everyone to hire me. But no one did.'

Ramy's mindset at this point is something all men with a family can relate to. It came back to the core concepts of masculinity to provide and protect. The only thing he could think about was how to earn a living for his family.

He went on Craigslist, applied for at least twenty jobs a day, and would get a few hundred dollars for filming a birthday party or something similar every other week. It was through one of these jobs that he connected with a friend of a friend of Nick Nanton, who is an award-winning documentary director. Nick had a cinematographer on a documentary shoot who had to drop out at the last minute. Ramy got an opportunity, did the documentary, and won an Emmy for it. A man is let down and another man gets an opportunity that changes his life.

Every time anyone asks Ramy how he is doing, his first response is, 'I have never been better.' The reality is that everyone wants to be with the happy person.

> 'They don't want to hang around a person that is complaining and whining about their life... be happy and people want to hang out with you.'

Happiness is not something you will gain once you have achieved your 'thing', but something you need to bring to your daily actions and attitudes. This is also why men need to talk openly about anxiety and depression, which is currently one of the biggest killers of middle-aged men. In the United States, men die by suicide three and a half times more often than women, and in 2016, 75% of all suicides in the UK were men. No matter how talented you are, how much you turn up, happiness can be the difference that makes a difference, and as critical as life or death.

Ramy is an example of a man shaping his environment, wherever that is, by his attitude, outlook, and the people he attracts as a result. He doesn't wait for success in order to have the 'never been better' attitude, and he maintains it when times are tough. We can all learn a lot from him; I know I have.

ACHIEVE

'If you want to achieve excellence,
you can get there today. As of this second,
quit doing less than excellent work.'

THOMAS WATSON, POLITICAL FIGURE AND PHILANTHROPIST

BEYOND COMPETENCE

ROBERT GREENE, USA

M any men are competent in their work – it is a given that if you choose to do it, you will be competent. However, you will not achieve your greatness if you stop at being competent in life; you need to go beyond to mastery.

Robert Greene is an American Author known for his books on seduction, power and mastery. He has five international bestsellers: *The 48 Laws of Power*, *The Art of Seduction*, *The 33 Strategies of War*, *The 50th Law* with the rapper 50 Cent, and, most recently, *Mastery*, in 2012.

Becoming a master in your field is to go through an apprenticeship and reach high levels of creativity. Robert emphasises that you can't have true success in your life unless you're good at dealing with people. People can be difficult, slippery and tricky… a bit like Robert's route to success. He had wanted to be a writer his whole life, but couldn't figure out what to write. He wandered, lived around Europe and in New York for five years, and tried his hand at almost everything, working in over eighty jobs on the way to mastery.

'I got a lot of knowledge and experience about people, which is really an apprenticeship for writers. I met a man in Venice who packaged books, sort of like a producer of books, and he asked me if I had an idea for... a book which I had never written before. In that moment, I just improvised. The idea would turn into *The 48 Laws of Power.*

'That was my moment of enlightenment. This is what I was meant to do. All of those bad jobs that I'd had, all of those ugly people doing their Machiavelli [Machiavelli is characterised by being amoral, subtle, cunning, deceptive and dishonest] and manipulations can all funnel into this 48 Laws of Power. It was sort of a magical thing for me that it all came together.'

To Robert, it felt like his one chance in life. The desperation, the sense of urgency, was what he calls in his book the 'death grab' strategy. When you feel that there's a mountain behind you and you have to fight the enemy, it's either conquer them fighting like a devil, or die with your back to the wall.

What is your death grab? Are you in it now? Have you ever been in a situation where your back-up plan is not an option? If not, why do you think that is the case? Do you need your own death grab scenario to advance as a man?

Robert's first book came out when he was thirty-nine. I'm thirty-eight now, so that inspires the hell out of me to get this book out. Get your 'thing' out there, no matter what your age is.

A lot of people give up too soon. Robert told me it took two or three years to build up steam before Jay Z was quoting *The 48 Laws of Power* in interviews and it ended up in the offices of many world leaders, selling well over a million copies to date. Robert was into his forties when his success really came to harvest after he'd been searching for so long and using his journey as a massive asset. I love that.

Opportunities come to us all the time. You'll meet people like the ones Robert met, and maybe you won't recognise them as an opportunity; possibly *the* opportunity. Are you prepared? Are you ready? Are you developing skills? Are you hungry for knowledge? Have you spent time practising?

'If you do that, something will happen, somebody will come. There will be an opportunity. If you're just a slacker smoking pot and dreaming about writing a great book, it will never come.'

I asked Robert what his definition of power would be.

'It's a degree of control. It's almost like a mathematical formula in life. We have very little control. We don't control who our parents are, what period in history we're born into, the historical circumstances, who we meet, and on and on you go in life. There's so little you control. Power is the tiniest of margins of control that you can bring about in life so that you have more and more control over circumstances.

'You control yourself, which is the major part of power, so you don't get so emotional or angry and do self-destructive things. With a mastery of yourself, you now have a slightly larger margin of control over circumstances and life. With knowledge and experience of what makes people tick, you can persuade and influence them better. Increase that margin of control ever so slightly until you know you have power. Just increasing that margin is what separates somebody who's helpless from somebody with power.'

The key to power is to know who you are. Awareness about yourself is so powerful that a third of this book is dedicated to it. Do you know what you want? Do you know what you're good at?

'You can bury yourself in your work and be really good at it, but you also have to work to understand people, the ability to get outside of yourself. I talk a lot about this in *Seduction*. A lot of guys are bad seducers because they're inside their head all the time. They go out with a woman and all they're thinking about is "Does she like me? Am I saying the right things?"'

If you're not paying attention in the moment, that carries over to all aspects of life.

THE 10 ALPHA LAWS OF POWER

Following my conversation with Robert and inspired by reading his books, I distilled some of his key concepts into 10 Alpha Laws of Power.

Law 1: Own your identity. Don't let others tell you who you are or what you are going to be. Take charge of creating yourself, your image, and recreating yourself as you continue to grow.

Law 2: Gravitate towards the happy and ambitious. People will be quite happy to tell you all about their misery every day if you lend them an ear. This environment is catching. You are a better contributor to the world if you are happy and performing to your potential. Avoid people who are generally unhappy.

Law 3: Reputation can make or break you. With a strong reputation, you are in a position of influence and positioned to win. Make it bulletproof and be proactive in defending it, as others will at some point attack it.

Law 4: Act it to become it. If you want to achieve a way of life, who would you need to become to achieve that lifestyle? What would they do and how would they carry themselves? Respect yourself and act as the man you want to become.

Law 5: Boldness begets boldness. Nothing great was ever achieved by timid or unsure action. If you are going to do it, go all in and commit to it. You can correct mistakes along the way with consistent action. If you are doubting yourself, do the work on yourself first.

Law 6: Don't isolate yourself. Be social. Communicate with like-minded people daily, whatever your location. Networks and alliances hold great power, so don't lock yourself away. There is protection in numbers.

Law 7: Tune into others' WIIFM (what's in it for me?). Put yourself in the other person's shoes, into their mindset, when you need to ask for their help. Don't drag up your past good deeds, as it can appear as if you only helped them out with a view to getting something in return.

Law 8: Deep focus. Don't be a jack of all trades, master of none. Find and focus your efforts on your strongest, most rewarding endeavour. Go deep in that area.

Law 9: Reassuringly ready. Opportunities are everywhere, but they all have specific and usually short-lived lifespans. Be ready to plant, cultivate or harvest, depending on the season. Don't appear to be in a rush; show patience, hang back when you need to, and know when to go all in.

Law 10: The value of free. If it is worth something to you, pay for it and invest yourself in it. 'Free' holds little value to the recipient and is usually laden with obligation. Have an abundance mindset; keep money flowing in and out. Generosity and investing in yourself are sure signs of an alpha.

ACTION 27: THE ELEVENTH LAW...

What would you add as a more specific key to your own power?

STILLNESS TO MOVE FORWARD

TOM CRONIN, AUSTRALIA

> '...established in being, perform action ...'
>
> **ANCIENT SANSKRIT, KNOWN AS 'THE MOTHER OF ALL LANGUAGES'**

Tom Cronin is a former financial trader who began work in a *Wolf of Wall Street* type environment in 1987. Characterised by greed, stress, drugs, unlimited expense accounts, this environment was where Tom eventually broke down.

He now spends a lot of time looking into the untapped human potential. He is the founder of The Stillness Project, focusing on meditation to combat chaotic, unsustainable and stressful lifestyles.

'I spent ten years in finance in a very stressed state and I spent fifteen years in finance after that in a very calm state. So, it wasn't finance itself or the job itself that was stressful. It was the way I related to it and the choices that I made while I was in it.'

That's the key point: stress is a response to a situation; it's not the situation itself. Many men try to seek fulfilment in a place where fulfilment doesn't exist. We may find short-term fulfilment, but it comes with a consequence.

'Every action has a corresponding effect. What I was experiencing was a negative effect because of the negative action. I started to experience a lot of anxiety, panic attacks, insomnia, depression, and my life just got worse. It was just chaos. If we have inner chaos, we are going to have outer chaos, and if we have outer chaos, we're going to have inner chaos.'

Most people change only when things get really uncomfortable. Stress, suffering, turmoil and chaos – whenever we have these symptoms in our lives, it is a message, a cue for us to do something different. Tom kept ignoring those cues and doing the same thing over and over again. The message got louder and louder until he snapped.

'I was a babbling mess. I couldn't stop crying, my body was shaking. I had no idea what was going on. I managed to crawl my way out the house to the doctor's and I thought I was dying, you know. I didn't know what it was, and when he revealed to me that I was having a nervous breakdown, I was like, "Dude, I'm Master of the Universe! What are you talking about? Surely it's my heart or something like that?"'

This was the severe wake-up call Tom needed. I can relate it to when I broke: the denial, to realisation, to surrender. Like me, Tom found the most demoralising aspect was having to face his deluded idea about who he was. In reality, he was just a crumbling wreck in a choice-less state.

'I could not possibly go another day doing what I was doing, and I had to make a change. That's when I started to look for other alternatives to the life that I was living. Once I started to find this inner calm, the choices I made were very different. I'd come off the end of a day's trading, I didn't want to go and get wasted, I really wanted to go meditate, go to a yoga class, to go surfing. I wanted to go for a walk in the forest and go home to see my family.'

I talked with Tom about tactics to create a life of reduced stress. Remember, we don't want to eliminate all stress. As men, we need a challenge – writing this book was ridiculously stressful – but we must be more resilient to anxiety and depression.

These are the top few tactics to implement:

1. **Learn to meditate.** This is the top priority. We can't make different decisions when we're operating from the same state of mind. It's important to spend time out in nature rather than processing data as often as you can.

2. **Cut back.** Many of us take on too much stuff. Tom's been meditating for twenty years, but he still admits to checking emails while he's stuck in traffic. I'm conscious about taking time out and structuring my day with gaps.

3. **Go to bed earlier.** Turning off all technology by 10pm is ideal for me. Your life will be different if you can consistently go to sleep between 10 and 11pm (adjust this if you plan to start very early the next morning). When I feel more stressed, this is usually the tactic I have let slip.

> 'If your goal is to get up early, your bedtime
> is actually the goal you're looking for.'
>
> **JEFF SANDERS, AUTHOR OF *THE 5AM MIRACLE***

If you think these tactics seem simple and obvious, they are. Apply them in isolation, or in combination for a more powerful impact. Which tactic can you commit to applying consistently in your life now? Even Tom doesn't think he's the meditation legend and stop because he's got it covered. It's a constant practice.

'Keep this thought handy when you feel a fit of rage coming on – it isn't manly to be enraged. Rather gentleness and civility are more human, and therefore manlier. A real man doesn't give way to anger and discontent, and such a person has strength, courage and endurance – unlike the angry and complaining. The nearer a man comes to a calm mind the closer he is to strength.'

MARCUS AURELIUS, ROMAN EMPEROR

ADVENTURE

'Life should not be a journey to the
grave with the intention of arriving safely in a
pretty and well-preserved body, but rather to
skid in broadside in a cloud of smoke,
thoroughly used up, totally worn out, and
loudly proclaiming "Wow! What a ride!"'

HUNTER S THOMPSON, JOURNALIST

THE HONEYMOON YEAR

I had always wanted to backpack around the world, but before I
knew it, I had a good, steady job, had met the lady of my life,
and I felt pretty set in the safety net of my little United Kingdom.
The wedding was coming and the to-do list was piling up. When
was I ever going to wander around the globe with all this going
on? Had I missed the window?

Hell, no!

My fiancée (now my wife) and I made a decision that really changed
our perspective on wedding planning. You can *easily* spend a year
in paradise (depending on what your wife is like) visiting twenty-
seven countries for as much as the average western wedding and
honeymoon cost.

Invest in your big adventures and relationships before you make
it to retirement (if you make it that far). A one-year honeymoon
is an extreme example, but life is an epic adventure or nothing.

Apart from the external experience, here are some of the internal values I discovered. This is what an adventure can do for your relationship.

Slow down to get on the fast track. You're guaranteed to have some quality one-to-one time with each other before the honeymoon phase of life moves on. This time will ultimately fast-track you to get to know your new wife on a deeper level, but so often, couples take one or two weeks for this process, then barely see each other afterwards because they both work demanding hours.

When you are committed to creating your ideal life, this total immersion is an efficient use of your time. If you discover the person you're with drives you absolutely insane, maybe it's time to fast-track the divorce process. A trip like this could actually save you ten or more years of your life.

Sharing a simple outcome. Each day, my wife and I had one clear goal: find what to do today for fun and adventure. This was the most consistently I have experienced living in the moment. I also enjoyed the build-up, having a simple, clear mission that we both shared and were committed to 100%: the tunnel vision and discipline to work, save, sacrifice and budget to achieve freedom.

If you and your partner don't share the same core goals, your relationship will not work in the long run.

Take on the world. The world is a big, awesome and sometimes scary place. Who knows exactly where and in what situations you'll find yourself?

When you venture into the unknown with your wife or partner, you really pull together as a team and look out for one another. You focus on what's important: adapting to your environment and getting back in one piece.

Prepare to fight? We had been told and almost convinced that we would have many arguments, being in each other's pockets twenty-four/seven.

The majority of couples argue over money, work commitments, paying the bills, and not making enough time for each other. All of these were non-issues on our honeymoon, so we didn't argue.

Relationships make the home. Our only constant for the entire year was each other. Whether we were freezing in a car in New Zealand or almost getting our tent trampled by a hippo in Kenya, my wife was there for me, and I for her.

People are the real value; you can make a home anywhere. You may be surprised by how little you need to be happy. When you are forced to fit your life and priorities into a backpack, this really helps you focus on what is important. Most off the stuff we have is rubbish accumulated over time; accumulate memories from your adventures instead.

The biggest eye-opener for me was how achievable it is to have an adventure. It doesn't have to be expensive, especially if you're a homeowner able to rent your property out for a year. Even without any other recurring revenue, we were lying on a beach in Ko Phi Phi, Thailand, having one dollar king prawn curry for lunch every day, and our bank account wasn't going down. Wait a minute – we could still be there!

The biggest obstacle that will stop you from doing something like this is the belief that adventures are for 'cool' people, but you couldn't possibly do it.

Or could you?

ACTION 28: EXPERIENCE

What is one adventure you must experience within the next year?

... Exciting, isn't it?

What do you need to make this happen? It may be simple, it may be complex, but damn, it's inspiring. (If it is not, at this point, you messed up, go back up to the question above and go again! The Silverback Moment coming up in this section may give you another idea.)

STAND UP FOR FULFILMENT

ROMESH RANGANATHAN, UK

I've known Romesh for a long time. We both taught at the same school, and then went on to different things. His impact on the comedy circuit since his debut in 2010 has seen him make a name for himself as a regular on national TV in the UK, working alongside many of the world's greats and culminating in him landing his own sitcom on British TV in 2018.

His story is inspirational in that he has been prepared to switch, no matter how far down another path he is, and not play it safe.

When Romesh initially got into teaching, he thought he'd had his 'awakening moment'. He had been working in finance for a couple of years, and remembers going to the toilets and crying for half an hour because the job was depressing him so much. He had to make a change, and made the leap into teaching.

'I'll never forget the first lesson I taught with this year 9 class [thirteen- to fourteen-year-olds]. If you could somehow channel the energy of year 9s into some sort of weapon, that would be incredible. I was stood in the classroom, setting up, and I was really nervous – you know what that's like. There was this little window on the door and they were looking in to check out their new teacher. You know the movie Jurassic Park when the velociraptors are looking through the glass? It was just like that, mate.'

He ended up being happy teaching maths, but had always loved stand-up comedy and thought it would be a great hobby. His mate was doing an open audition for a competition and told him to come along.

Romesh ended up getting into the final of the competition, where one of the judges came up to him and said, 'You know, you could definitely do this as a job.' He remembers thinking it seemed such an unusual job to do. But an unorthodox path gives you experience. You become 'uncopyable', with a unique point of view.

We talked about the self-doubts Romesh had, especially in the early days.

'The difficulty of comedy is you always feel like you're pretending to be a comedian, and somebody is going to tap you on the shoulder and say, "Mate, we know. You wanna just cut the act."'

When we start anything new, we are at our worst in terms of ability and confidence to perform. The only way to get through this is by action, and it can be painful to get over the hump. Think back to the premeditation of evils exercise, imagining worst-case scenarios. Romesh told me about a time that really fits the bill. Let's just say it didn't quite go as he'd hoped.

'At that stage I had only done short sets, and I was booked by quite a big promoter to do half an hour and I was nervous about it. It was in this theatre in Essex, but it wasn't in the theatre itself. They had cleared the foyer, set up the chairs and it was about a hundred people. So, I thought it was funny to say, "It would have been nice to actually be in the theatre, why are we in the foyer?"

'Anyway, it turns out they really liked that foyer. It was the first thing I said; they hated it. They basically thought that this guy that they don't know has come in and insulted their foyer. That got absolutely nothing. I then, honest to God, I performed to complete silence for half an hour. When I finished, they didn't even applaud. You can hear the mic click back into the stand. One of the worst experiences I've ever had in my life.'

Failure can be subjective and excruciating, but it has to be moved through if you're striving for something that inspires you. Life is difficult enough without doing something that you don't enjoy. All of us have self-doubts. Many people I have interviewed have talked about the 'act it and become it' mentality. Act today as the man you want to become. Eventually, you'll fool yourself and you'll be that man.

'Beyond being funny, with comedy – and teaching – people have to want to spend time in your company. Like they want to be listening to you or working with you. If you lose that then there's nothing you can do.'

What Romesh has achieved is inspirational to me (especially as he's from my home town), and this book had to have at least one comedian in it to remind us not to take life too seriously.

RAINBOW ROAD

'Imagine you're chasing a rainbow every day.
You got to the end and found there was no gold,
just an empty pot. That was my life. Where do you
go from there? You have got to start creating or
that pot is not going to be full when you get
to the end of it. You have to fill it.'

TIM MONTGOMERY, FORMERLY THE WORLD'S FASTEST MAN

The approval of others means you're really achieving some serious success, right?

Most of us are taught to strive for approval by teachers, parents and society. As we grow older, this benchmark can mix us up when it comes to achievement, freedom and fulfilment.

Each man possesses both creative and destructive forces – the Ying/Yang of life; inward motivation and outward appearance. We are all pulled and pushed by opposing forces to varying degrees. Do you act out of inspiration or desperation? Do you have the ideal job or lifestyle for you, or by society's standards? Should you settle for what you have achieved or are achieving as it consistently meets the approval of others? More importantly, are you doing something worthy of your own respect?

If you avoid responsibility for your actions, or hype your actions so they appear greater than they are, that is a sure-fire method to create an empty shell of a man.

ACTION 29: RESPECT

- What do you do that you respect yourself for?
- What do you do that you do not respect yourself for?
- What (else) would you have to do to be worthy of your own respect?

Stop being a guy you do not respect. Are you rigging the game against yourself? If your answer to the third question above is to be 6 foot and you're a fully grown man of 5 foot 9, you will never respect yourself, but so long as you haven't put something delusional, read your answer again. Imagine you have already achieved it. How would you feel? Take time to go through the emotions in detail. That's what you're going to get, so now go and do it.

You must respect yourself as a priority. Fulfilment is an art; it is different for all of us, and it is the master skill of life.

THE SILVERBACK MOMENT

The mist was rising from the dense jungle that covered the mountains. We were deep in Africa, near the Uganda–Rwanda border. Getting to the area had been a bit of a mission, having rocks thrown at our truck, and now we had armed guards to keep us company.

As we approached the base of the mountain, the terrain became steep and muddy as the jungle closed in on us. Pretty soon, we couldn't see more than a few feet in any direction, and a machete became a necessity. In front of us we had a day's trek to find Charles and his family.

Charles was a local 440lb mature silverback gorilla who was about to kick our arses and remind us who's boss. I'll share what I gained from the experience so you don't have to risk getting squashed by a gorilla (although I highly recommend the adventure).

Be prepared to roll with the punches. We had been told we might see some gorillas from a safe distance, and that they would likely be taking it easy. The reality was that when we stumbled across the gorillas, they were not taking it easy. As soon as we found them, we were on their terms, and they were ready to remind us of that.

So many people like to schedule and plan everything down to the last detail. We attempt to control others and the situations we find ourselves in to fit our agenda, but sometimes we just have to prepare for the unknown. Gather the theory, but be ready to adapt to what is in front of you and enjoy the ride.

Don't be afraid to get out there. No matter what the guidebook said about the gorillas or what they were generally observed to do, we would never have had a balanced or rounded knowledge of them without coming face to face with one. Nothing could beat getting out there and actually applying what we had learned.

Learn to experience the real world, not just from reading about it, but from getting your butt out there. You'll learn more about what you desire and, ultimately, yourself.

First impressions matter to a gorilla. We had the honour of having an awesome bloke from New Zealand with us: a big rugby-playing guy who didn't think things through. He was wearing all black with his hood up, and he could easily have doubled as one of the gorillas. As a group, we were pretty sure that if Charles didn't have a fight with him, he would adopt him.

Think about the signals you send out and how you present yourself on a daily basis. Take a moment to assess new environments you may be going into and the impression you will make.

Reactions to an angry silverback vary. We had all been given a safety briefing and we knew exactly what to do in the 'unlikely' event that a gorilla would charge at us, but it was a different experience out there on the mountain. We found the group of about twelve mountain gorillas in dense jungle; my first glimpse was a baby gorilla crawling at my feet.

We could see Charles the Silverback's giant head as he sat slightly down the mountain. Myself and two other bright sparks thought it would be a great idea to get a bit closer to him, so off we went. I was behind the other two, and as you do in these situations, I slipped and fell forward, knocking into the other guys.

As I looked up, the first thing I saw was Charles thundering directly at us. Two of us got our response right: we made ourselves look small and puny, we looked down, etc. Unfortunately, the third did completely the opposite. He jolted up, eyes wide, arms up, and the charge continued.

At about three feet away, Charles veered off to the side and past us. Exhale. He grabbed the baby gorilla and flung it in a bush, strutted around a bit, showed us who 'The Daddy' was, and generally looked pleased with himself.

You learn how you instinctively react when you're under pressure only through experience. Sometimes, what you *actually* do can be quite different to what you know you *should* be doing, so put yourself outside your comfort zone on a regular basis.

Know when to walk away. Once we had all survived the charge and a 'scuffle' with the other gorillas, we were tempted to carry on spending time with them. As scary as it was, it was also great. However, the mood these gorillas were in, they were clearly telling us something. If Charles charged at us a second time, he would most likely follow through.

When great or exciting experiences happen, we can sometimes fall into the trap of always wanting more. The result is we become less fulfilled in that moment, as if two of something will automatically double your experience. One plus one does not always equal two.

This experience ultimately reminded me to treat each day as an adventure, a bonus. I accept that you are unlikely to get charged by a silverback and beaten to death with your own arm, but you never really know what is around the corner.

SUMMARY

'Mountains know secrets we need to learn.
That it might take time, it might be hard, but if
you just hold on long enough, you will
find the strength to rise up.'

TYLER KNOTT GREGSON, POET AND PHOTOGRAPHER

- Become the man you want to be now; claim his actions, behaviours and associations

- Stop actions and associations that prevent you from embodying the man you must become

- Develop your presence and ability to communicate powerfully

- Develop control of your state and apply the keys to increasing your power

- Stress is your response to a situation. You decide on your response and take the necessary actions

- Decide on exciting adventures that inspire you

- Do things worthy of your own respect and align with others on a similar mission

CLOSING ACT

'Strange, isn't it? Each man's life
touches so many other lives.'

CLARENCE THE ANGEL, *IT'S A WONDERFUL LIFE*

In the final section of the book, I'll be asking you to think about some brutal realities.

- What are you doing with your life?
- Why are you doing whatever it is you are doing?
- What are you sacrificing?
- What legacy are you currently leaving?
- What legacy do you want to leave?

There is also a sobering reality for all of us in the last exercise.

LEGACY

CREATE YOUR RIPPLE

When you make improvements, tweaks, change yourself for the better, do not underestimate the effect it will have on those around you, and beyond. Everyone creates a ripple in this world; that is not a choice. What is a choice is whether it's a negative or positive ripple.

On the most basic level, when you go for a walk, you either smile at people you pass, or say hello, or ignore them, or stare at them as a show of force. Whatever you choose will ripple on to the next person, and the next and so on.

It is far too easy to get caught up in the pursuit of the alpha in the common areas of money, career, status and possessions. I am sure you would achieve success in your chosen arena if you focused only on that area, but at what cost? Will you have a positive impact? We are the sum of all parts of our lives.

If I could show you the formula to a stress-free life, how good would that actually be? It would mean eliminating all of the negative experiences in life, and how realistic is that? What would that achieve? Would that make you happy? If all stress is eliminated, you will permanently be in your comfort zone. Is that thriving? What kind of legacy would you be able to build and leave?

'It is one thing to not be overwhelmed by obstacles, or discouraged or upset by them... But after you have controlled your emotions, and you can see objectively and stand steadily, the next step becomes possible: a mental flip, so you're looking not at the obstacle, but the opportunity within it.'

RYAN HOLIDAY, AUTHOR OF *THE OBSTACLE IS THE WAY*

As humans, we need challenges, both physical and mental, to test our mettle; to strengthen; to develop; to feel fully alive. There really is no light without the dark. Would I wish for some of the traumatic things that are going to happen to you or me? No, but they *will* happen at some point. These are the times when you need to battle for your alpha and overcome your own adversity.

ARE YOU TESTED?

ALPESH PATEL, UGANDA

I first spoke to Alpesh in 2014 about how he had taken on the world's mobile phone giants as Africa's first home-grown mobile phone company, Mi-Fone. He was the first man I had back for a return interview in 2017, and a lot had changed.

Alpesh has truly been tested as a man. He was born in the jungle of Africa, and was to become one of the original refugees to be kicked out of Uganda by General Idi Amin back in the early seventies. With little warning, Amin ordered all Asians to leave Uganda 'or else' within a ninety-day period, going on a rampage of brutality, murder, rape and reported cannibalism. Luckily, the British government took Alpesh and his family in.

'Adam, I really did take on Africa and Africa gave me a serious hiding. Even though when we exited the business, we sold to a massive company and it was a success.

'When I originally left Motorola at forty having generated around $500 million in sales for them, I thought I was the slickest guy on the planet. I thought I knew everything. The minute I decided to jump off that cliff and build a plane on the way down with Mi-Fone is when I really learned about myself.'

Over that first six or seven years, Alpesh produced revenue of more than $40 million, his phones sold in seventeen countries, but he could not figure out why Mi-Fone was not able to raise money. He was frustrated to the point where he was close to giving up when a $5 billion South African conglomerate approached him, wanting to buy part of his business.

Alpesh had been all over the world looking for money, and the money was actually twenty minutes down the road. How many times have you assumed you have to look far beyond your doorstep when the gold is right in front of you?

But that was just the start of a challenging deal for Alpesh. The conglomerate spent one year on due diligence when it was meant to take just three months. Finally, the day came when the documents were ready, but by that point Alpesh didn't have enough money to pay his lawyers.

'I was really desperate because I had assumed that the money would have come in after three months, and when the deal came on the table, I had to stop trading. I became my own lawyer as I did not have $200,000 for lawyers' fees.'

The deal was all set and agreed. Then at the last minute, the conglomerate pulled out. Alpesh received a call saying the CEO who had organised the original deal had resigned.

'That night I cried. I was in real pain and I didn't know what to do. They had the power, they could have walked away from the deal, they do deals every day. I was cornered into a stage of desperation. I had already exhausted my other options; I didn't have any other options. With the delay of the deal and ceasing trading, I was stuck.'

Over the next three days, Alpesh managed to convince the conglomerate's board they needed to go ahead with the deal. It was one of the few times in African history that a start-up has gone from nothing to being acquired by a $5 billion publicly listed company.

'I signed the deal and it was an amazing feeling. Unfortunately for me, that feeling did not last long. I didn't really like what happened afterwards. I had post-acquisition blues.'

Fulfilment is not a straight transaction. From zero to hero, and then what? His company had been his baby and his mission for nearly ten years, and now Alpesh had lost control. Decisions that used to take five minutes now took four weeks.

Due to the time the deal had taken to finalise, getting back into the market proved tougher than both Alpesh and the conglomerate had expected. Africa was in recession, and a Chinese brand called Xiaomi had come in with handsets almost identical to Mi-Fone's. The Chinese phone was literally destroying Alpesh's brand, and the African governments were allowing it to happen.

'For me, I think it was my final straw because I realised that no matter how hard you work, no matter how above board you are, in Africa there are no rules. That really tested my mettle, and while this is all going on, I'm still having this challenge of building the business again.'

Lost momentum is huge in everything.

'Even though we put some money in our pocket, what did we really give up? Was it worth giving up what we had? Entrepreneurship is very glamorous right now. The problem is that the grass is not always greener on the other side… and if it is, it's probably fertilised with bullshit. Some people have very good jobs; entrepreneurship is not for everyone. If you have a great job, you enjoy it, you can spend weekends playing golf or whatever, you have time every night to hug your kids, that is a great position.'

The art of fulfilment is something all of us must work to master. When you take on a challenge like Alpesh did, it can become all consuming. He told me it was hard to turn off and relax when he did get any downtime, especially in the last year.

'I've become a much more spiritual man. If I can be a better man tomorrow than I am today, I'm making progress. Stay in your own lane.

'What sometimes frustrates entrepreneurs is we're always waiting for some external people or forces to help us. We're waiting for this guy to give us money, waiting for this guy to give me an order, this guy to perform. We are all at the mercy of external people. What happens is that messes with you because you get frustrated. Now imagine where you accept the fact that there are external forces that you simply can't mess with.'

From the moment we're born to the day we die, we face a series of tests. Some we will win, but the majority we will fail. Be fully aware of that when you're going into challenges and deciding whether to test yourself. Don't let one or ten failures knock you off your stride; learn, adjust, apply and go again.

'The only way to know how strong [you are]
is to keep testing your limits.'

JOR-EL, PLAYED BY RUSSEL CROWE IN *MAN OF STEEL*

MAN IS MEANT TO THRIVE

Men will do whatever it takes to provide the basics and survive. The problem is once we are surviving, many of us will stop doing the daily work needed to continue advancing, gradually falling back down towards ruin, and then the cycle repeats itself.

This cycle can also be true when you move above surviving to thriving. If you stop the discipline, drop some or all of the habits that got you there, you'll fall straight back down to surviving, or worse. I have done this so many times.

Man is meant to thrive. Imagine if you continued with as much energy, perseverance and conviction as you need to avoid ruin. This simplicity combined with discipline will create your freedom. I have talked a lot about you, your mindset, what you need to do to claim, create and lead your ideal life, but it is not all about you. If you just focus on yourself, at some point you will come unstuck. Be sure to focus on something bigger than yourself.

'At some level we know that the more we
focus on the self and our small, singular story,
the more lost we can become.'

DR JOHN IZZO, AUTHOR OF *THE PURPOSE REVOLUTION*

When we're focusing on others, it becomes about more than just what we have to lose if we stop, give in to resistance or break our moral code. Others are now affected by what we choose to do, and throwing in the towel begins to feel pretty self-centred.

That said, let's remove any idealistic notions that there are men who do everything in this book all the time and never make mistakes, get frustrated or doubt themselves. That is not me, and unless the sun shines out of your arse, that is not you, either. It comes down to how we navigate the stormy and calm waters alike. When we're under pressure, it is easy to stop thinking of others; to adopt a 'me, me, me' mentality. In survival mode, economic or otherwise, we need to maintain our will, our guiding principles, just as when we're thriving. As impactful men, we always need to be in training mode, so when adversity comes, and it will come, we are ready to battle for ourselves and others.

If you're struggling and feeling down today, one of the most effective ways to feel better is to help someone else with no ulterior motive. Of course, don't only do this when you are feeling crappy; it is a positive lifestyle choice you can make anytime. On a larger scale, it is why a mission that is not just about you is so powerful.

The Japanese concept of *ikigai* is a combination of the words *iki*, meaning life, and *gai*, meaning value or worth, so *ikigai* can be translated as 'reason to live'. The pursuit of *ikigai* is definitely something that inspires me, and it will likely inspire you, too. It is enlightening both in finding your way, and in reassessing when you feel you have lost your way.

It may also help in clarifying your mission, which brings us back to where we started in this book, which also emphasises the cyclic nature of awakening your alpha.

ACTION 30: *IKIGAI*

Draw the above diagram as large as your space permits. Leave room to 'brain dump' yourself, your essence and what you are currently doing or want to do. Play around and put in things that feel a bit 'out there' to you.

This exercise will help illuminate your *ikigai*. You may be living it now, or it may become clear what you need to do to take your life to the next level. Either way, both these scenarios get me ridiculously excited.

THE MINI-ME MOTIVATOR

'A king, realizing his incompetence,
can either delegate or abdicate his duties.
A father can do neither.'

MARLENE DIETRICH, ACTRESS AND SINGER

As a man, becoming a father is a game changer. Now a new relationship is born. Little eyes are watching us constantly. They observe how we react to life, and more importantly, how proactive we are; how we choose to lead our lives. Everything we do, good or bad, is amplified.

The relationship you form to produce a son or daughter is crucial, so pick your partner wisely. How do you treat your partner? Is it a loving, understanding relationship that you both work at to grow together? If your relationship is toxic beyond repair, do you now show your children it is not OK to settle with the wrong person? By being strong for them, you will make them, and yourself, develop in strength. When you're leaving a legacy, the number one thing you can achieve is to raise strong sons and daughters to have a positive impact on the world. I have been writing this book with that squarely in my mind.

'My father didn't tell me how to live;
he lived, and let me watch him do it.'

CLARENCE BUDINGTON KELLAND, WRITER

There is no tomorrow.

Just hold that thought; let it sit for a minute; absorb it.

This has always meant something to me (hell, it's from *Rocky III* for starters). Basically, get things done, now. It's why I abandoned my plan B to launch the podcast. It's why I have written this book.

If, for whatever reason, there is no tomorrow for me, how will I guide my sons? How will I offer them advice daily on a range of random and relevant topics? They will have over 300 episodes of their dad 'jibber jabbering' (as they would say) on audio via the podcast, going through key life lessons, asking questions of various inspiring people. They will have this book to read when they are ready, and more importantly, when they choose to – as you have chosen to read it. I plan to do so much more to have a greater impact, but if this book gets anything across to you, I hope it is this:

Plans alone accomplish nothing. So, what are you going to do?

YOU ARE NOT DEAD YET

'My dad had wanted to write books, he wanted to
have a radio shop. That's what he really wanted to do,
and he said, "I'm going to do that when I retire."
But he didn't live that long.

'A lot of people said to me, "Wow, starting
your own business was really brave." It was naïve
at best and stupid at worst as I hadn't got
a clue what I was doing.'

DAVID SHEPARD

A lot of people put their dreams on hold, but you can't count on having time in the future. My friend James Butler (man on a mission) knew this, and now he is not here to read these words. We all must embrace this fact; we must understand the damage a mentality of 'I'll do it tomorrow – someday – when I'm ready' has on our lives and our loved ones.

ACTION 31: YOU'RE DEAD

There are many versions of this powerful exercise out there, but all follow this basic concept.

Imagine you are looking in on your own funeral as you currently are. You can see everyone who is there: all your closest friends, family, colleagues, and even some surprise people from your past have shown up. At this funeral, they are all going to speak about you. What would they say?

You are still looking in as they talk about you at the bar afterwards. What stories would they tell? What legacy have you left? What would your impact have been? Think deeply about this as it is your current eulogy. Some may be tough to hear.

Now what do wish your eulogy would actually say?

That kind of thinking helped me in writing this book. I was wrestling with what to include, how to approach it. I was planning, thinking about several other potential things down the line. Then I stopped myself.

This could be the one book I ever get the chance to write. This ultimately could be the final piece of my legacy. My will strengthened to truly be in that moment, to not hold anything back, to create something that is a real reflection of what I believe will be of service and have an impact (if applied).

How is the world different because you are in it? What is or will be your positive impact? What is your legacy? What are you going to be known for? How will people remember you?

Your legacy is based on today, every day. If that thought makes you feel uncomfortable, a little panicked, or fills you with regret for all the things you haven't done yet... good. That pain, that level of discomfort is what you'll need to make significant changes. If you were to die tomorrow, it must be with no regrets about how you chose to lead your life today. Our future is not guaranteed, and it is defeatist or cocky to think otherwise.

If you did know when your last day would fall, whether weeks, months or years from now, would it change the way you are choosing to live your life in this moment?

If the answer is yes on any level, decide to make the necessary changes to become the man you want to be now and live that life. Commit to *Awaken Your Alpha* each and every day, to rise up...

You're not dead, yet.

THE 25 MOST IMPACTFUL BOOKS

We are all standing on the shoulders of giants and this list is likely the most valuable resource in the entire book. Those of my own top ten books that made the list are marked with an asterisk. If any catch your eye, this is a great place to start. For full lists and more of my own recommendations, connect with me at www.ayalpha.com.

I put this list together from the 337 recommendations for 195 different books that I've received from over 300 podcast episodes over the past four years. The 25 books below were suggested three or more times, and I've listed them in ascending order of popularity.

BOOKS SUGGESTED THREE TIMES

Byrne, Rhonda, *The Secret*

Canfield, Jack, *Success Principles*

Ferriss, Timothy, *The 4-Hour Body*

Godin, Seth, *Tribes*

Hill, Napoleon, *Outwitting the Devil*

Kiyosaki, Robert, *Rich Dad Poor Dad*

McKeown, Greg, *Essentialism*

Peters, Steve, *The Chimp Paradox*

Ruiz, Don Miguel, *The Four Agreements*

BOOKS SUGGESTED FOUR TIMES

Frankl, Victor E, *Man's Search for Meaning* *

Hendricks, Gay, *The Big Leap*

Keller, Gary, *The ONE Thing*

Olson, Jeff, *The Slight Edge* *

Pressfield, Steven, *Turning Pro*

BOOKS SUGGESTED FIVE TIMES

The Bible

Carnegie, Dale, *How to Win Friends and Influence People*

Cialdini, Robert, *Influence*

Gerber, Michael, *The E-Myth*

Greene, Robert and 50 Cent, *The 50th Law*

Pressfield, Steven, and Coyne, Shawn, *The War of Art* *

BOOKS RECOMMENDED SIX OR MORE TIMES

Deida, David, *The Way of the Superior Man*

Ferriss, Timothy, *The 4-Hour Work Week* *

Maltz, Maxwell, *Psychocybernetics*

Robbins, Tony, *Awaken the Giant Within*

THE NUMBER ONE MOST RECOMMENDED BOOK

This book was recommended twice as many times as its nearest rival:

Hill, Napoleon, *Think and Grow Rich* *

ACKNOWLEDGEMENTS

There are so many people who helped in getting me to this point, and for that I thank you. I would particularly like to thank those who had a direct impact in making this book a reality:

First and foremost, my wife Christina for her support in understanding the book's importance to me and for being flexible and resilient with me through the many deadlines of this process. Without our teamwork, this book would have broken me. I love you for who you are.

My sons, Dylan and Harrison: as men of the future, you are my muses. When writing got tough and thoughts of quitting tried to sneak into my mind, I knew I could not let you down. You were always asking about getting 'copy number one', and that kept me going. Our many play and 'bundle breaks' were essential, too.

Mum and Dad for asking the simple question 'How's the book going?' on our almost daily Skype calls. Teaching me that all I can do is my best, you strengthened my resolve to get this book out there without holding anything back.

The readers who gave their feedback at an early stage when the book was still forming: Tim Dixon, Jack Turner, Ryan Black, Ben Short, P.J. Dixon, Paul Edgewood and Greg Rollett. This was a scary threshold for me to cross, but you delivered the goods I needed to get the book to where it is today. You all helped make it better.

The guests from the podcast, with special mentions to James G. Butler, Travis Jones, Craig Ballantyne, Tim Montgomery, Brian Grasso, Lance Allred, John Blake, Silvio Simac, Charlie Brenneman, Matt Lovell, John Romaniello, Cole Hatter, JV Crum III, David

Shepard, Nick Unsworth, Toby Alexander, Ramy Romany, Tom Cronin, Romesh Ranganathan and Alpesh Patel. Also, to the listeners of the podcast from over 130 countries: I know you're out there and I appreciate you.

Kavit Haria for your professional and personal companionship over the past few years, including during my transition across the Atlantic. There have been ups and downs, but the faith we have shown in each other is special, and I do not take that for granted. To me, it is no coincidence that our books will be published in the same year, and I cannot wait to read yours.

Robert Greene for the inspiration to use years of research and adversity to produce my first solo book at thirty-eight years young, and for setting the bar high in your mastery. I have often thought of you reading this book, and that strengthened my resolve to continue upping my game.

Hans Zimmer for your genius musical compositions which have served as my soundtrack to get me in the zone.

Arnold Schwarzenegger for your inspiration and entertainment over the years. Your bold declarations which you have followed through from an early age have had an impact on me and this book.

My publishers, specifically Joe Gregory, for your patience, belief and understanding as I worked through the many challenges to get this to print.

Finally, every reader of this book. I want to get to know you better, so please reach out. Take a photo of yourself with this book wherever you are, share it across social media, tag me and *#AwakenYourAlpha*. Your individual support will have an impact.

THE AUTHOR

Adam Lewis Walker is a lifestyle entrepreneur, high-performance coach and keynote speaker. He is also the host of the top-ranked podcast *Awaken Your Alpha*, interviewing the world's elite in over 300 episodes since 2014.

A former teacher and international pole-vaulter, Adam was attempting to reach the Olympics in 2008 when his career was cut short by a freak accident. During the following two years on crutches, trying to cope with the realisation he would never compete again, Adam hit rock bottom. He had to rebuild his dreams and identity, eventually fighting back to represent Great Britain in a Paralympic sport and refocusing to help others achieve, regardless of their obstacles.

In 2013, Adam co-authored *The New Rules of Success*, sharing his no-nonsense approach to health, family and leadership. The success of this bestselling book led to the creation of *Awaken Your Alpha* and Adam's quest to share inspirational stories, strategies and insights to becoming the leader in your life. As a coach and mentor, he works to cultivate the mindset needed for excellence and fulfilment with an alliance supporting action, accountability and adjustments to enhance legacy. As a keynote speaker, Adam gave the TEDx talk *Awaken Your Alpha, How to Rise Up* and has been featured in *The Huffington Post*, ESPN, PodFest, Influencers Radio and many other media outlets.

He is a proud parent to Dylan and Harrison with his wife Christina. Originally from West Sussex in the south of England, Adam recently achieved a lifelong dream to move his family to the United States.

TAKE ACTION

For continued inspiration and consistent application going forward, join Adam and his guests every week on the top-rated *Awaken Your Alpha* podcast for ongoing tales and tactics to thrive as a man.

To instantly dig deeper into the book's actions and apply them with more impact now, I invite you to the accompanying comprehensive course at www.AYAlpha.com/course. Here I walk you through the steps to take in detail and go beyond what I could fit in the book. This, together with the associated coaching and Mastermind programme, delivers unique support and structure for growth.

You can subscribe to the podcast on iTunes or Stitcher, and you can access all the resources at www.AYAlpha.com

CONTACTS

www.AdamLewisWalker.com
www.AYAlpha.com

🖼 | 🐦 | 📘 @AwakenYourAlpha

🖼 | 📘 @AdamLewisWalker

in www.linkedin.com/in/AdamLewisWalkerUK

✉ AdamWalkerUK@me.com